WHEN VILLAGE BELLS WERE SILENT

The author writes:

It's natural, I suppose, even at the very eleventh hour before the start of another great war, to stop and think among the growing lambs, the bronzing plum trees. I remembered Milton's

'How soon hath time, the subtle thief of youth,
Stolen on his wing my three and twentieth year.'

Back on the farm I drove forty lambs to market that autumn of plenty. Skipper, my wall-eyed blue border collie, zigzagged behind the snow-white flocks much like a cyclist climbing a hill.

We brought the lambs in unsold at one pound a head and turned them on the hill to winter. We little knew then that soon we would be queueing at Evesham for the scrag end of mutton.

So came the last week of 'peace in our time'.

When Village Bells Were Silent

Fred Archer

CORONET BOOKS
Hodder and Stoughton

Copyright © 1975 by Fred Archer

First published in Great Britain 1975 by
Hodder and Stoughton Limited

Coronet Edition 1977

Printed and bound in Great Britain for
Hodder and Stoughton Paperbacks,
a division of Hodder and Stoughton Ltd,
Mill Road, Dunton Green, Sevenoaks, Kent
(Editorial Office: 47 Bedford Square, London WC1 3DP)
by Hazell Watson & Viney Ltd, Aylesbury, Bucks

ISBN 0 340 21810 X

CONTENTS

ILLUSTRATIONS

Between pages 80 and 81

ACKNOWLEDGMENTS

1 Gerald Warren

2 Keystone Press Agency Ltd.

3 Len Bayliss

I

The Last Year of Peace

WHEN NEVILLE CHAMBERLAIN RETURNED FROM Munich holding that piece of paper with Adolf Hitler's signature, what did we think, living in this green Paradise under Bredon, yet so near to the possible 'Hell' to come? What did I think as the words 'Peace in our time' rang out over the wireless that autumn in 1938?

'It yunt worth the paper as it's writ on,' Jim Hicks said. 'Old Hitler's a just playing for time. Time to tackle we lot, you can't appease a fellow when power has gone to his yud.'

*　　　*　　　*

As winter closed the brussels sprouts dropped their leaves like half-open umbrellas. They looked sad those frosty mornings until the weak rays of the sun melted the ice and soaking wet we walked the three feet alleys between the rows picking the sprouts into the nets.

The news seemed brighter, but Will Richardson quoted from the Bible as we talked to each other over his overgrown hedges saying that things were like they were in the days of Noah, feasting, drinking and getting married, but the day of doom was near.

Will never married, but was in love with Bredon Hill as real and as true as if she were a buxom country maid. Will studied her curves, her changing face, as a lover would the girl of his choice.

Men were leaving the land to build the 'Aschurch Camp', double the wages for less than half the work.

Short of labour that winter to dig the long alleys of asparagus with the two-tined (or pronged) fork, Walt and I struggled with a little Ransome plough and two horses to mould the asparagus beds up.

'Master job I ever did,' said Walt on those never-to-be-forgotten Friday pay nights. 'It ull ruin the grass (the asparagus) ya know, Gaffer, and don't that make my arms ache trying to plough that clay on to the top of the beds. 'Tis sidelon, ya see, it unt level.'

We finished the job one sleety day in February when the horses' manes were white with hoar frost by afternoon. Then the sun went down like a waggon wheel behind the Malverns and back in the Tythe Court orchard the first lamb was born.

I penned the raddled ewes in the thatched sheep barn at the edge of night while the hurricane lamp swung from a plough trace near the lambing pens. As the timbers creaked in the old barn where Roman numerals marked the joints on the beams I sat on a kerf of hay until a plaintive bleat came from one of the flock. Quietly I walked among the ewes, they were pulling the sweet hay from a wooden hay rack. A cry came from a ewe.

'On a-lambing,' Jim said.

What a thrill to see the forefeet first, then the nose, as the ewes strained until the lambs lay wet and yellow on the clean straw. I carried the lambs to a prepared pen hurdled like a private ward. It was a private ward in the rough-and-tumble maternity home of the orchard.

Faces as white as snow the lambs inherited from the Ryland tup. Our Ryland tups, natives of Herefordshire, were short in the leg, white in the face, compact and very good for crossing with the Kerry and speckle-faced ewes to produce early lambs.

'A mangold, do you fancy?' I said to a ewe. She first licked her two lambs then scrunched her teeth into the winter delicacy of mangold-wurzels, as sweet to a sheep as Cox's Orange Pippins are to mortal man.

The lambs came thick and fast, the ewes looked kind and healthy, their udders or bags hung dripping with milk. Then disaster struck. I noticed some lambs with diarrhœa badly. I drenched them with a mixture prescribed, no-one then had much knowledge of lamb dysentery, no injections then; quite a number died like flies in winter.

'Them as keeps hosses must expect losses,' Tom Wheatcroft, our cowman, said.

In spring I finished with an average of a lamb and a quarter per ewe. There should have been more.

The early fat lambs went to the butcher weighing thirty pounds dead weight at a shilling per pound. Not a fortune, but times had been worse.

The news that summer on the radio was gloomy. Hitler's promises looked like being broken. The village woke from its long sleep of optimism as first-aid classes began in case of air raids.

We came away from the school after our last lecture with certificates.

It seemed to me so much like the storms up the Severn Valley; it looked as black in the papers as they did over Gloucester. Then the clouds parted over the Cotswold Edge and the Malverns; we once more saw the sun.

'Didst yer old Hitler a-ranting and raving on the wireless last night?' Jim Hicks who worked for Sammy Bosworth at No Gains Farm asked me.

'Yes,' I nodded.

'Balling he was like an old cow on a bulling,' he said.

In May and June the asparagus crop was as Walt had forecast, the buds were, as he said, like parish churches one in place.

'The ground's as full of switch grass as hell's full of parsons,' Skemer Hill confided in me. So we decided to plough the field ready for autumn wheat.

'Dost remember Jingler Jarvey as had the small holding at Hill Withy?'

'Just,' I told Skemer. 'He was the man who went to market in smart breeches and leggings and drove a fast mare. Did he grow asparagus, Skemer?'

Skemer sucked breath through those ill-fitting stained false teeth of his, raised his eyebrows and said 'Oi'.

I knew that Skemer Hill had a story to tell and egged him on a bit.

'What happened to his sparrowgrass?' I said.

'The sparrowgrass beds was wore out, oi, nigh on twenty years, and he wanted to sell the ground just as the feow buds was peering through. And they was a feow, I can tell ya. Jingler went to the market the day before the sale and bought some hampers of sparrowgrass buds. He poked um in his beds so that the buyers as come to buy the ground thought they were buying a useful piece of sparrowgrass with the land. He got away with it. You know, Fred, honesty *is* the best policy, but it keeps ya devilish poor.'

Skemer spent that last summer of peace burning sparrowgrass roots as he called them.

Village women who had been through the 1914 war were busy bottling plums, pears and making jam, and some of the farm workers bought a pig just in case of a shortage.

I had a late piece of hay up in the Langet, an awkward field on the hill belonging to a likeable character known as Laughing Tom.

After it was cut by my brother's Fordson, I raked it with Tom the nag into walleys or windrows ready for the pitchers.

It was hot and sticky that early August night when I got home sore from sitting all day on an iron seat. Over a cup of cocoa and bread and cheese I switched on the wireless.

One of Hitler's speeches was being relayed. I rather liked listening to German, it seemed so similar to Welsh, but this was different. Hitler appeared in an ugly mood over something; his voice was the voice of anger threatening a certain storm. 'Sabre rattling' some called it. Then the response of a crowd full of emotion answering with their *Heils* again, not unlike some over exuberant crowd. Did Evan Roberts carry the Welsh miners in this manner in his religious revival, I wondered?

There was a difference, of course—Hitler carried a crowd full of ambition to be the master race and himself to be another Napoleon, while Evan Roberts' theme was brotherhood love. In those last days I wondered why after so much success without much bloodshed the Dictator should have a lust for yet more power.

The B.B.C. bought Wood Norton as a safe place six miles away, plans were afoot for evacuation, the papers were full of rearmament.

Once more the land was going to be vital for our survival. Every ounce of grain, every potato and apple would be wanted to feed us if and when Hitler tried to expand still further.

Since Dad's illness a year before that last summer of peace I had taken over 150 acres of the farm while my elder brother farmed the Old Manor. For brothers we were so different. Tom was keen on the fruit and vegetable side of agriculture and the marketing of these crops, always eager to try new methods. To be honest he had a flair for business, I didn't even drive a car; until the war began I was still going to market with a horse and dray. Sheep and cattle were almost everything to me. A good rick of hay and a bunch of fat lambs pleased me more than all the onions, plums and sprouts in the Vale of Evesham.

I did say these things were almost everything to me, but

Saturday nights at the Scala watching Will Hay or Carmen Miranda with my friend Frank were quite pleasant.

One Sunday night a party of young people from Cheltenham came to our Chapel. They included a girl of about eighteen called Janet Henry, she had won cups for her singing at festivals and the like. She sang that evening. It's hard to remember the piece, but the chorus included these words, 'I believe I belong.'

Janet was plump as a puppy, her voice rang as clear as a bell.

Goodness, I was slow, always expecting things to happen without any effort on my part.

In the post one morning a card arrived with words under a picture of a horse race; a horse race — well, Fred Archer the jockey. The words sunk in at last. In everyday language I got the message:

'You have won my heart and you are the one for me.'

Slipping the card in my working jacket pocket I wrote to her and arranged a meeting on Saturday night. She worked until about seven, my bus left at ten. She talked a lot about the St. John Ambulance Brigade to which she belonged. What had I to say? A bit about sheep perhaps, but I thanked her for the card and told her she had a lovely voice.

This sort of thing must have happened to millions, but I had the feeling that in my case it was different, no-one ever felt like this before. Was I in love?

It's true it was pleasant to be in each other's arms in the darkness of Sandy Lane.

I was naïve, but Janet was what Jim Hicks would have called 'Not yet dry behind her ears'. I kissed her lips; very pleasant but just no response.

I suppose if I'd kissed away all the lipstick off her chubby face, she would still have held me loosely with her back to the five-barred gate.

She invited me to meet her parents. Back at her home I met the smell of beef sausages and chips. No five-star hotel ever put on such a spread as Janet's mother. Just superb. What a kindly woman — only I wasn't looking for a mother-in-law but a wife.

The Saturday meetings became weekly events. Janet's Dad
had served in the Horse Artillery during the 1914 war. Over the
sausages and chips he relived his active service with knives, forks
and spoons. We set the battlefield on the clean white damask
tablecloth. Mr. Henry put the fish slice where his gun carriage
was in position. The horses were restless. Mr. Henry with his
comrades drove towards the enemy lines, then laying the gun in
position the team of horses wheeled in an arc and, knowing the
danger of No Man's Land, galloped hell for leather for the British
lines.

Mr. Henry tugged the tablecloth as if it were his reins. He
pressed his knees against the sides of his chair as if the whole
thing was being fought all over again.

'Once, Fred boy, a small shell burst wounding the horse beside
mine.' He explained how quickly he unhitched the leather
covered traces, led the dying animal to the roadside ditch and
shot him with his rifle.

Yes, Mr. and Mrs. Henry were kind to me, but somehow I
don't think that Janet found me an ideal consort.

After walking a mile from the bus stop at 11.30 p.m. my mind
was soon back among the farm animals. Was Ada, one of my
cows, going to have a heifer calf? Would there be any sale for
sprouts on Tuesday, a by-day at market? Days went by full of
the wrestling with heavy soil, chasing wayward sheep, mending
fences. I'd think of Janet towards the weekend and wonder
whether she would have a headache and be unwilling to walk up
the slopes of Leckhampton Hill and view the Cotswolds from
The Devil Chimney, or was I going on another Royal Horse
Artillery charge with Mr. Henry, whose photograph graced the
piano. A photograph of a youthful soldier in putties with spurs
on his boots.

At the piano Janet sat playing and singing Sankey's hymns. She
had been converted, could give her testimony; she would be a
good influence on me, she told Dad. Dad just smiled. I'd seen
converted folk and some were changed for the better while some
put away their religion with their Sunday clothes.

After a while Janet and I parted as the threat of war became more real and who knew, I'd possibly be drafted abroad in khaki, navy blue or powder blue.

Mother wept as mothers do and forecast that I'd pick up with some butterfly or other. Mother had been a Sergeant Major, a young people's Sergeant Major in the Salvation Army. (That's a Sunday School teacher if I must explain to those who have no idea of the complexity of Nonconformity.)

It's natural, I suppose, even at the very eleventh hour before the start of another great war, to stop and think among the growing lambs, the bronzing plum trees. I remembered Milton's

'How soon hath time, the subtle thief of youth,
        Stolen on his wing my three and twentieth year.'

Back on the farm I drove forty lambs to market that autumn of plenty. Skipper, my wall-eyed slate-blue border collie, covered many more miles than the three the country road signposted. He zigzagged behind the snow-white flocks much like a cyclist climbing a hill.

I walked in front and stood at the crossroads to persuade the forty to keep straight for market. Really there was no need to stand in the gateway to the field of green sprouts; Skipper sneaked ahead and lay bellied between the posts waiting for the last lamb to pass, then back again zigzag behind.

We brought the lambs in unsold at one pound a head and turned them on the hill to winter. We little knew then that soon we would be queueing at Evesham for the scrag end of mutton.

The story was told in the days when we were queueing up for everything that some locals saw the sign up 'Tales from Hoffman' and queued expecting a bit off the meat ration (Offenham being in our Vale) instead of the rich music of the composer across the narrow sea.

But life had been kind to me. With 4 pound notes in my pocket I felt rich so I bought a chalk-stripe suit from Dunn's at Cheltenham, a good-cut material for fifty shillings. Then a pork pie hat in nice velour, a pair of synthetic fur gloves for twenty-five shillings. Extravagant but they lasted for years.

After long hours in the sheep pen, smelling of Jeyes Fluid and Stockholm tar, with trousers stiff with the lanoline from wool it was good to get away on Saturday nights. These veneers as you might call them were the outside of my life, the front turned to the world. I had my secret thoughts deep in the spirit, the soul, or whatever name you choose to call it by. I believed then as I do now with my whole heart and soul in the indestructibility of life and spirit. When we drop the book or lay down the pen we cannot drown the echo of the heart, there is no end, no beginning to it all. A man does not write a book simply to amuse himself or fill in his time. There is a real attempt in doing so to win the inner peace of the spirit. Maybe this should be resisted; it's not the goal, perhaps, but a reward which fulfils a need in me. However selfish it is, one does like to be made to purr sometimes. It's good to live again, looking back over the shoulder at the mistakes and missing in a real sense voices now silent.

So came the last week of 'peace in our time'. A baby was born to be a granddaughter to our stockman. I waited in the road while my old friend Tom Wheatcroft called to see the new arrival. I remember holding two bikes outside the cottage door as Tom came out chuckling after he had told the nurse how soon his latest in the family line knew how to put her thumb to her nose at us old craters.

As Sunday morning dawned I walked up our village. On that September morning life was as usual. The folks at the top end of the village walked to the bottom to Church, the folks at the bottom end walked up to the top to Chapel. That's how it always seemed—a meeting and saluting and raising of hats by people of different denominations. I saw Ralph walk past with his violin in the black case, upright and smart in navy blue, to lead the singing at the Chapel Sunday School as he had done since before I could remember.

At eleven we listened in to the B.B.C. The expected words

rang out. Neville Chamberlain's voice was full of emotion. No one commented much. It seemed that the inevitable had come.

After Sunday dinner the sun shone hot for September. The ditches and ponds were dry. My store cattle in the Middle Dewrest had circled the field all the morning with tails erect as if it were July.

They pushed under the willow branches by the muddy pond, stood in the water. First one and then another broke through the fence into the adjoining meadow. I cycled down the lane with Skipper and drove them back through the gap, carrying a couple of withy poles and stakes to do a temporary repair to the fence.

Almost wellington-deep in mud I shovelled away at the pond, our drinking place, until the shovel scraped the stone bottom. The water from the spring which fed the ditch trickled into the drinking hole until it ceased to be like cocoa and became drinkable for the heifers. They stood around me like women round a pram. I stood back with Skipper. They sniffed at the water, drinking deeply that hot afternoon; the stronger ones slid on the slippery decline of stones and drank first. I waited until tea-time and drinks had been had by all.

I thought that if the rain didn't come soon the heifers would have to leave the meadow where the brown blossoms of the wild white clover and the fawn and faded Timothy grass were palatable on dewy mornings and the shade of the withies was a refuge from the flies.

Monday morning came with speculation by the veterans of the 1914 war. Some said it would be over by Christmas, one man whose geography was not a strong subject told me not to worry about the Germans because we should stop them 'coming up the Suey Canal'. Howard Cambridge, who was later our Chief Air Raid Warden, had had a brick air-raid shelter built in his garden, the steps were all ready to enter this first attempt by a man of Ashton to provide a shelter wired for electric lights. He laid in store a certain amount of essential rations. A reinforced concrete slab covered the underground cave which lay like a flat tombstone in some village church of centuries ago. It lay in between two rows of asparagus, now in fern covered with red berries.

2

If Winter Comes

'IF WINTER COMES CAN SPRING BE FAR BEHIND?' A SEVEN-year-old evacuee from the Black Country read these words poker worked on a wooden picture on our kitchen wall.

Harold was one of forty or so who had come to Ashton-under-Hill village to shelter from the threat of German bombs in the industrial Midlands. A chubby little lad who, like the rest, soon brought the words 'Aw' and 'Yaw' to our little village school.

Ashton folk were a bit stunned when the coach arrived bringing the children, but soon all were billeted in the no mains, no sanitation houses and cottages in this West Midlands community.

Conversation in the village during the first weeks of war was centred on the children.

'Poor little mites,' Jim Hicks said, 'to be brought yer from the town so young, brought yer from the lighted windows, the cinema and the shops. 'Tis alright for the likes a we,' he said, 'as bin allus used to the water drawn from the pump or stand pipe, and the bucket closet, and some on us ain't got the 'lectric, just oil lamps.'

Two young militia men had joined the forces and this and the blackout were the only real signs that a conflict was under way in Europe.

As Harold and his friends walked up through the orchard heavy with apples and pears they formed a crocodile with their teachers on the nature walks towards the hill. Windfall apples crunched under their feet.

The sleepy September wasps bored holes in the mellow pears. Harold thought 'Caw, we never sin the like Dudley road!' The Saturday market was the nearest place Harold had been to any fruit and then it had to be paid for.

'Don't thee give our two vaccies any more pears, ull ya, Fred, if you please,' Jim Hicks asked me at Chapel one Sunday night.

'Why, Jim?' I said. 'They seem to like the mellow Burgandies.'

'Certain they do,' Jim raised his eyebrows. 'But it makes work for the missus, they messed their trousers again last night.'

I thought how when we were boys the green apples of August never seemed to upset our insides. Of course we had been weaned on them, and the Black Country lads had never eaten fruit so fresh and free before.

It's a thought how soon children adapt to changed conditions. In no time at all they were eager to feed the fowls, lead horses, drive cattle and sheep, and here as in other rural areas town and country mingled at school and in fields and at play.

Climbing the trees with the village children and picking the late blackberries was second nature.

The next crop to fall on the autumn orchards was the green-

hudded walnut. These were sought after every morning before
stained little fingers went to use the pens at school. Stained by
the green huds which came off the brown walnut shells like
taking skins off bananas.

Then came the weekend bus from the Black Country with its
load of parents and older brothers and sisters of the new country
children. It parked outside the Apple Tree pub. Before Sunday
dinner many of the munition makers of the Midlands had drunk
the Apple Tree dry.

Some Ashton housewives were waiting with warmed up
Sunday dinners for their guests. Two images emerged: firstly the
anxious mother who had worried all the week over Johnny at
Ashton. The air-raid siren had gone often at his home town
where his mother had run for shelter. At least Johnny was safe
at Ashton, safe from the bombs. Then there was the father who
looked on Sunday as a day to sample the country ale, away from
his noisy machine. Surely a stimulus to his war effort.

Like other children the evacuees were full of mischief.

'They be allus busy,' Jim Hicks declared. 'Too busy when they
lets Mrs. Bosworth's geese out of their pen, when they looks
up her hen eggs. Luckily I spotted the geese gwain up the hill on
the edge of night, the gander in front. They walked like a team
of horses, and it's likely, you know, Fred, that Master Reynard
the fox would have come out of the coppice and bang would
have gone about twenty Christmas dinners.'

'Oh yes, the fox would have put paid to that lot.'

I saw the village children doubled in number in a week. Then
came other folk to take refuge among our hills and orchards.
Every cottage was full of 'people from away', as they were
called. The Manor became a kind of boarding house in our No
Man's land.

The women folk joined the W.I., the children gathered rose-
hips for syrup and weighed down the grammar-school bus.

The difference was so sudden. Before, every furniture van
which unloaded or loaded was noticed, everyone knew everyone
else, and a great deal of their business. The whole village knew

the children's birthdays. Now life at Ashton had changed because of this influx from town and city, but it was so necessary.

Sammy Bosworth's young hopeful Ernest, the seven-year-old son of a steel worker, was unsteady on the bucket closet seat among the nut bushes at No Gains Farm.

Climbing up like a perched hen, his feet nine inches off the blue-bricked floor, in the words of Jim Hicks, 'The poor little bwoy had had a miss deal.'

Following Ernest on that autumn morning Sammy Bosworth, unbuckling his broad leather belt, made his way along the path and into the privy. 'Come here!' he shouted as the little boy ran through the rickyard. 'What's the meaning of this? Our seat is meant to be kept clean, do you hear me?'

Ernest looked crestfallen as he stood by Jim Hicks. Jim halted a minute with a burden of hay on his pitchfork on his way to feed the calves.

The boy looked up at his guardian and quietly said, 'I'm sorry, Mr. Bosworth, but I hadn't got my glasses on this morning.'

'If that unt the licker,' Jim muttered as he went to the calf pen. 'I'll be damned, they has to wear glasses to go to closet in the Black Country, and many's the time I goes when the night's as black as the ace of spades.'

One thing that interested me about the evacuees was their instant curiosity about the countryside and its folk, the flowers, crops, animals and birds.

The boys and girls who lived near the village cross came to my cowshed after school time when I was standing watching the calves suckle the nursing cows.

It's an eternal cycle rearing calves. The calves suck the cows who adopt them for three months, then comes the weaning; more calves are bought from market and some cows kick at their newly adopted sons and daughters. Some won't let the milk down, resulting in a deal of bunting at the udder by the suckling calves.

The evacuees asked if they could squeeze a cow's tits to make the milk come. They squirted milk from my old quiet cow, pointing the teat at their friends, and assured me that their milk came in clean bottles.

'Has a bull got tits?' one bright boy asked me.

Before I could reply his brother said, 'Don't be so daft! If you see a cow with a bunch of hair under its belly that's a bull.'

'What are bullocks?' one ten-year-old asked me. 'Are they young bulls?'

Sitting in the manger with a stick just to threaten Darkie, my only Friesian, who was kicking at a week-old calf I'd fetched from Gloucester the Monday before, I said, 'Go over to the yard, look over the gates, there are the bullocks.'

Frank and Ernest, who lived with us, called me Uncle.

'Uncle, can I ask you summat?' Frank said, holding up his hand as if he were in class.

'Go on,' I said.

'Well,' Frank stuttered, 'I've sin Mister Bennet's bull and he got a big heart between his back legs. Your bullocks got no heart.'

I looked at the boys who were so eager to know the facts of life and told them that to stop them being fierce, most bulls had an operation but it's not the heart that's taken away but something else.

'Coo,' Harold said, 'fancy cows having operations.'

'Bulls, ya daft thing,' another boy chimed in, 'and any road our Mum had a hoperation.'

'I've had me tonsils out, see,' Ernest chimed in.

I felt that they were learning at first hand from the cowshed as I had done when a boy, but that these boys had been sort of thrown in at the deep end.

They came from the brick, concrete and chromium plated shops and cinemas to a different world. A village where the blossoming of spring would be come and gone before they could take it all in, and where winter was a mixture of slush, frosted greens, frozen taps and Wellingtons.

3

The War Agricultural Committee

IT WAS PRETTY OBVIOUS THAT OUR SYSTEM OF FARMING
in 1939 would not do for wartime. Acres of land just grazed a
few sheep and the wheat grown in our parish only amounted to
a few tons.

A County War Agricultural Committee was formed with its
various officers, some in charge of a pool of farm machinery, of
drainage and ploughing up the pasture land.

My belief is that our county was singularly fortunate in its
officers, men who had practical farming experience and forward-
looking men from Agricultural Colleges. This didn't apply to all

counties; if you read in Mr. Wentworth Day's book *Harvest Adventure* a chapter called 'Little Hitlers on the Farms', you will read of injustice on a big scale in some of our eastern counties. Some committees he refers to had among their members unscrupulous landlords, dealers, jobbers and farmers who had failed in every district.

A District Officer was head of a District Committee. This system was in the main very good because it meant that a district member controlled three or four villages where he farmed himself and knew the land.

George Cowley, our representative, was a retired farmer of about sixty-five and lived quite near.

At the beginning of the war the obvious flat pastures had to be ploughed up and planted with wheat or some other food crop.

Orders were served on farmers, who agreed with the local representative as to which fields he would plough. The big snag was that the small farmers were not geared for arable farming. They had no tractors. Tractors could not be bought without a permit and a long wait. This created a situation where old tractors at farm sales made more than the new price. But if necessary the War Ag. would plough and plant the land, and in fact did so. Their drivers worked long hours ploughing land which had been grass since the Crimean War.

Jim Hicks was dubious about the War Ag.

'Stands to sense,' he told me, 'fellas from our County Town — "Townees" I calls um — can't farm by looking at books.'

I knew Jim well and could understand his feelings.

'Now look yer, Fred,' he said. 'That damn great yalla caterpillar tractor has started to plough our gaffer's best grazing ground, Merrylands. Twelve acres of the best turf in the county, but the clay is ploughing up as hard as hell's bells. What um gwain to do with it?'

'Disc it, I suppose,' was my answer.

'If the old Squire had been alive he would shot um. Where's Master Bosworth going to put his cows?'

I walked with Jim to Merrylands and saw the land being

ploughed. Jim looked on in disgust and was almost in tears as he spoke loudly to me against the din of the crawler tractor.

'I've had baskets full of mushrooms on dewy August mornings out of this medda.'

'Jim,' I said, 'the tractors are working in the Green Thurness, that field of mine near the road. Mr. Cowley suggested I ploughed it for wheat.'

Jim cleared his throat and as we walked away he told me that I'd never see another pasture like that in his time.

'It takes years to make a turf,' he said.

'Have you ever heard of Mr. George Stapleton?' I asked Jim. 'He's had a lot of success ploughing old pasture and reseeding it.'

'No, but I've seen cattle grazing on this reseeded pasture and there is no holt nor stay in the grass. It goes through their bellies like a dose of salts.'

We went home.

Tom Wheatcroft, who worked for me, had the same theory about old pasture but reckoned that the Green Thurness would grow wheat.

'I suppose you ull plant Square Heads, Master?' he said.

'No, the War Ag. advises Holdfast.'

'Can't beat Square Heads, Master,' Tom told me. 'But what be ya going to do with it now it's ploughed? Disc it, I suppose, both ways, up and down and crossways.'

The tractor driver disced it, then Tom harrowed it with our two horses and got a reasonable seed bed.

'It wants a good rolling,' he told me then. 'The ground's like a woman, it wants squeezing and squeezing tight. That helps the crop against wireworm damage.'

Meanwhile Thomas Bennet, the Birmingham ironmaster who had bought Partridge Farm, had enough implements to farm his 450 acres without the help of the War Ag. machines.

Henry Fanshaw, his bailiff, had just married Flick, the daughter of a local vicar. They lived at Rosemary Cottage.

Henry was out early in the morning immaculate in leather strapped breeches and a hacking jacket to meet his men. Bert

Amos was in charge of his Suffolk horses. Ralph Sims caught rabbits, mended the fences and made gates. Young Syd Freeman drove the tractor. Then there was Charles Stephenson, cowman, Walt Gillet, shepherd, and Bill Brown.

Some of Partridge Farm was too steep to plough, but Mr. Bennet was a good businessman and agreed to plough every acre George Cowley asked him to.

This was the way of our War Ag., they did ask first, and if another field was offered as alternative arable, George would usually agree.

'Have you heard about Master Fanshaw as went to one of our agricultural colleges?' Jim Hicks asked the locals at the Apple Tree pub. 'Oi, he wanted young Bert Amos to go to Ernie's, the saddler's, to get some bigger collars for the hosses.'

'Why?' asked Cedric Richardson, the smallholder from The Needlelands.

'The silly fella was trying to put the hosses' collars on without turning them the other way. It stands to sense they wouldn't go over their yuds.'

'That's education for ya,' Jim laughed, and told the story of what happened during the last war when some chap from the town sent the women to pinch the runners off the dwarf beans and of course they grows no runners; unt that why they be call dwarfs?'

Cedric Richardson, a bachelor of thirty-eight, had two meadows. One he mowed with a one-horse mowing machine and made a little rick of hay. The village lads helped him to get it together on his light four-wheeled dray. The other field his cows grazed.

Cedric was what Jim called 'an afternoon sort of fella', never getting up much before dinner time. His brother kept some laying hens and a few turkeys. They lived off the land as his family had for six hundred years, milking his one cow for the house and rearing a few calves. His Cheviot ewes were more often on the railway line than in the meadow.

The fact was that Cedric's family had been a part of the village scene for so long they were accepted. That slightly eccentric way of his had been the result of intermarriage, but there was an air of breeding about the man. His lips, which seemed perpetually to hold a long-ashed woodbine, were surrounded by a ginger stubble. Hatless, he drove his cob and float through our village. His blond long hair was bleached by sun and wind. Cedric appeared to me the last of the pure Saxons.

'The War Ag. has instructed me to inform you that you must plough up one of your pasture fields, Mr. Richardson,' George told him one day as he stood in his Cotswold-tiled cowshed while two calves sucked the last drop of milk from one of his cows.

Cedric grinned, maintaining his freehold, and offered to show George Cowley his deeds.

Now George Cowley was a reasonable man and knew that the field lay wet in the winter and was in fact land below the level of the brook.

He had seen the field flooded for weeks on end. He went back and reported to his District Officer that Richardson refused to plough his meadow but somehow he didn't blame him. It was useless to plant corn there until the brook was cleaned out and the land drained.

We knew only too well in the country that when the Ministry of Agriculture in London demanded so many acres of corn to be grown, the onus was on the Executive Officer of the county to get the job done by the farmer or the War Ag. George Cowley recommended that Richardson's fields were better left as pasture, but that he should be what was known as a Schedule C farmer and put under the War Ag.'s supervision so that his land would be stocked by more cattle and fertilised to help food production.

But the Executive were adamant and after due notice sent a tractor and ploughed the land. Cedric was furious. 'This treatment,' he said, 'after six hundred years in the village as a family.'

He threatened the War Ag. tractor driver with a slasher or hedgehook. P.C. Wood was called, an order for dispossession was served and Cedric had to sell his cows and give up his land to the War Ag. P.C. Wood issued a summons for assault on the tractor driver which meant that Cedric was fined £10 and bound over for a year.

The dispossessed farmer walked to the market town, paid his fine in golden sovereigns. 'Some of his grandfather's,' Jim Hicks said, 'they was as black as the ace of spades.'

It must be emphasised that a dispossession order in our area was only implemented on this occasion. We who were natives and knew Cedric's background were sorry. Jim Hicks and Skemer Hill agreed that 'Thee canst grow nothing on water-logged ground, only water cress.'

The winter wheat planted by the Committee came up bright and green in November.

'Thee wait until February Fill Dyke when the brook meadow be up to yer ass in water,' Skemer said.

I smiled and knew what he was going to say.

'Oi, that wheat will go as yellow as a guinea then. The roots are deep in water and then if it freezes its goodbye to the War Ag. wheat.'

Young Eric Packer, who worked for me, pulled Skemer's leg and said the War Ag. might have a new sort of wheat that grows like rice in water.

Skemer sucked his breath as we stood on the headland, and his false teeth rattled.

'You talk as yer belly guides ya, and it udn't a done years ago in the Squire's time,' he added.

The obvious did happen. The wheat on Richardson's land failed, but Sammy Bosworth's grew a good crop at No Gains Farm.

Mine in Green Thurness was quite good, but Tom Wheatcroft was right, the ground wasn't firm enough, and on the headland he pointed out to me how good the crop was where the tractor turned and firmed it.

'You remember what I said about wireworms?' I nodded. 'Well, just look here,' and in patches the wheat in the spring had gone a yellow colour and picking hold of the blade it could be pulled rootless from the ground.

'That's wireworms,' Tom said. 'Always the same on fresh ploughed turf.'

Tom laughed and said, 'It was a fairish crop, but don't forget what I said about the land and the women, they wants a squeezing hard.'

As we rode home on the dray pulled by the brown cob, Tom asked, 'When's that tractor coming as you ordered, Frederick?'

'What you want is another couple of young horses,' said Skemer.

Eric Packer looked at me and said, 'Skemer's past it. I'll be glad to see the Fordson tractor.'

'What the Hanover's holding it up?' Tom asked me. 'Master Bennet has got another new one. Daresay he pulls some strings in Brummigum.'

'It's got to come through the War Ag.,' I said.

'I got no faith in them,' Skemer replied. 'We'll soon have to get permission to dig the taters in the garden.'

Meanwhile Cedric was out of a job, and went to work for Sammy Bennet; well, that's when he felt like it and that suited Sammy.

That autumn Thomas Bennet's orchards were laden with plums, pears and apples.

'That's the result of a good dressing of potash to the roots,' Henry Fanshaw bragged as he drank his beer in the Apple Tree pub, 'and our potatoes on the hill look promising.'

'How many backhanders does your Gaffer give the merchants for all that bag muck?' Jim Hicks was anxious to know.

'"Cos it's all on coupons allocated fair, so they says, but money ull talk. Take that new tractor of thine. I suppose Master Bennet shared a bottle a Scotch along the 'secutive officer of the War Ag.'

'I must away,' Henry said. 'I have a heifer calving. Good night.'

'Good night to you, Henry. Dost want me to come along in the morning and show a hagricultural college chap which way to put the hosses' collars on?'

All in all Mr. Bennet's bailiff did grow some good crops for the war effort at Partridge Farm. His college training stood him in good stead, but he did not have the advantage I had of being steeped in the soil, neither had he learnt the art of listening to and watching the old hands at their work. This I found most important. Tom Wheatcroft was an invaluable source of information on crops and stock.

At Partridge Farm Bert Amos was eager to show Henry how things should be done, but the bailiff felt it necessary to plough his own furrow in front of Mr. Thomas Bennet.

We in the village were so fortunate in having George Cowley as our War Ag. District Committee man.

Dad took over the care of two villages as War Ag. representative, and in one case where the farmer was old and his land poor he was eager to give up. Here the War Ag. tractors ploughed the ant-hill covered, rabbit-infested pasture and with persistent cultivation grew good crops of wheat on the heavy, almost blue clay.

Bulldozers pushed up hedges. Combine drills sent here from the Commonwealth sowed seed and fertiliser together.

A farmer nearby had orders from the War Ag. to plant fifteen acres of potatoes.

By December the potatoes had not been dug, and here we got an example of local administration being more efficient than the land being ruled from the County Town, or even worse, from Whitehall.

Joe Smith had jogged along for years, just he and his wife on a cheaply rented farm. Half the farm had been overrun with hawthorn; he had made enough money to live comfortably without working full pressure. His corn crops he had ricked and some he had thrashed, but potatoes on that clay were an alien crop.

Frank Bell, the District Officer, reported the fact that Smith's potatoes were in the ground at Christmas.

Dad went to his District Committee meeting where the County Executive Officer was present. Here the officer made an order that the potatoes were to be dug within three weeks or Joe Smith would be dispossessed of his 250 acres.

From Christmas Day until late January it snowed and froze every day. At the next meeting the Executive Officer asked Dad if Joe Smith had dug his potatoes, and of course being a committee man responsible for Smith's farm, Dad had been over there the day before and seen the sorry state of the potato field, so he was obliged to report that things were the same as at Christmas.

The Executive Officer with his sheaf of official papers in front of him on the desk looked at the ordnance map and said, 'Well, gentlemen, we must dispossess Mr. Smith from his farm for not complying with committee's orders.'

Dad, who had farmed clay land since he drove a four-horse team at plough, rose from his chair and put one question to the officer:

'Could you have cleared or organised the clearing of fifteen acres of potatoes these last three weeks of frost and snow?'

The other farmer members of the committee, including George Cowley, agreed that it was impossible.

The order was never made. Dad drove over to Smith's farm next day, to tell Joe that the War Ag. were after his blood, and that as soon as the weather dried he must get his potatoes harvested at all costs.

Joe complied and wrote to the War Ag. telling them that he would vacate the half of his farm overgrown with hawthorn if his landlord would agree. The landlord did agree. The bulldozers went in and cleared the thorn. The War Ag. squad then burnt it and the land was ploughed and planted.

It takes a war some say to revolutionise farming, but revolution can be so dictatorial, so lacking in local commonsense.

Of course Joe Smith should have harvested his potatoes earlier, but when he did the crop was light, the land was so unsuitable. It's a fact that is often not recognised that the soil varies so much from field to field.

It is so easy, I know, to criticise the system and I believe the

War Agricultural Committee was a good force in food production, but the local committee members who were farmers or ex-farmers were invaluable in making it work.

Cedric Richardson's little holding was a case of officialdom carried out to the letter. It left its mark: Cedric from the day of dispossession was a changed man, a broken man in many ways. Yes, he died soon after with a broken heart. The field lay like a flooded sepulchre to him.

The corn failed every year. The War Ag. seed was wasted on boggy land.

As the convoys lengthened along our main road, the ditch became a hazard to the inexperienced lorry drivers. Every day or so the breakdown army lorries were there with their men pulling some truck from the ditch which was the source of Carrants Brook. The Council did the easiest thing by piping the ditch with huge concrete pipes.

There seemed no time to deepen the watercourse before the pipes were laid and the land levelled and covered with chippings.

Yes, it saved the lorries from being ditched, but the pipes blocked the water from the field ditches although junctions were placed where the drains from my land emptied.

Drainage officers were a part of the make-up of every County War Ag. One came to me with his ordnance map.

'I can send a team of men out,' he said, 'to dig your ditch deeper and drain your neighbour's farm.'

I looked at the plan and rode in his car to the place where my pipe ditch emptied into the council's pipe. Here lay about two feet of water unable to get away because the council pipe was not low enough.

'Fifty per cent subsidy I can offer you,' said the Drainage Officer, 'and our men will make a good job.'

'It's no good,' I replied. 'The water can't away.'

I fetched Tom Wheatcroft.

'What's the problem, Fred?'

'The Drainage Officer suggests lowering our ditch.'

Tom cleared his throat, climbed down to the water's edge and looked at the levels. He cast a wily eye up the ditch, then at the pipe.

'I'm not going to say that you drainage men can't drain land. Oh no, but not in this case because neither you nor Winston Churchill can make water run uphill.'

I suppose our part of the country was a difficult one for controls to be enforced.

We had so many little men engaged in agriculture and horticulture, men who to my mind were the salt of the earth. These growers and small farmers knew every inch of their holding. They knew that some land grew asparagus well, some would not. They studied wind and weather as their fathers had. It's these men, who have been despised by various governments, who really produce quality crops, fruit and vegetables in particular.

Let me mention one. The War Ag. declared that for every acre or part of an acre of spring onions grown the grower must produce the same acreage of what we call harvest onions. The bulbs with golden skins for drying and for lasting the winter. These onions were needed badly by army camp canteens for stews, etc.

Spring onions, before price control, rocketed in price so it was a temptation for the growers to pull all onions green for sale instead of harvesting them.

George Cowley and Dad in our village knew that this was being done by one or two who were on the make, hurrying to get the good market price. It did mean constant watch on some growers who were tempted to pull all the crop.

Jim Hicks, who now helped on Sammy Bosworth's farm with the brother of the late Cedric Richardson, was appalled at the practice.

He was, in his own words, 'ashamed of the way the onions be gwain to market in forty-pound nets. Mind tha',' he told me, 'and as much dirt in the net as onions. 'Tis no good on. I worked years for a market gardener and was useful making the small bunches of onions tied be the women into packs of a dozen as I stood in the shed be the bench. They tied them with withy or osier twigs, then washed them in water tank until the roots was as white as snow, then put um to drain and packed them in hampers. Slovenly, I call it, besides it unt honest selling so much soil. No pride in the job now.'

I asked him what he thought of it all in general.

He said, 'Well, the War Ag. got good intentions, but folks round yer be a cashing in on shortages.'

'What do you mean, Jim?' I said.

'Well, the other wick l was in the market and some fella had sent into the sale a trailer-load of crow onions.'

'Crow onions,' I said, 'you mean what grow in the wheat and come wild round our hedges?'

'That's the gospel, as true as this fork's in my hand' (he was planting his garden potatoes).

'Stunk,' he said, 'they stunk the market out, and I was glad the auctioneer refused to sell them. Why, bless the fella, one of them with your bread and processed cheese as they calls it would take all the breath from your body, and if it didn't do that your tongue ud burn like fire. The missus told me the other day, when I mentioned it to her, that there was more in my yud than the comb ud take out.'

'She's right,' I said, 'I reckon you ought to be on the War Ag.'

It's true Jim Hicks and his local knowledge would have been useful to the War Ag. The tragic episode of Cedric Richardson would have been averted. I felt that Cedric's loss to our village was irreparable. His family and mine had worked land on either side of the hedge for so long.

'Surely,' I told Jim and Sammy, 'this war was being fought against dictatorship and here we were, faced with the end of Needlelands Farm.'

The Cotswold stone cowshed where Cedric milked his cows, made his rick of hay, was levelled to make a road for War Ag. machines to enter the ten-foot gateway.

Living as I did in a close-knit community where once Cedric's father was a guide and counsellor to us all, I felt that Goldsmith had seen in 1770 the real threat of such dictatorship in the decay of peasantry. In *A Deserted Village* he wrote:

> Ill fares the land to hastening ills a prey
> Where wealth accumulates and men decay.
> Princes and Lords may flourish or may fade,
> A breath can make them as a breath had made.
> But a bold peasantry their country's pride
> When once destroyed can never be supplied.
> But times are altered, trade's unfeeling train
> Usurp the land and dispossess the swain.

With the dispossession of Cedric, a gap was made, a wound which festered among the old folk until at last they went.

It was not all gloom these little bureaucrats brought in their train, for didn't they entertain us with howlers?

'What dost think about Joe Smith's bit a fortune?' Skemer hissed through his teeth one morning, and turning to Eric he said:

'Thee tell him, Eric, thee knowst more about tractors than me.'

Eric was doubled with laughing as he explained to me that Mr. Smith had put in his application for petrol to start his old Fordson tractor. In the form it asked 'What other means of transport have you on the land?' 'One gelding,' Joe Smith wrote on the form and damned if they didn't send him coupons for ten gallons for the tractor, and an extra six gallons for the gelding.

Skemer looked over his steel-rimmed glasses at me and sucked more air between his badly fitted khaki teeth.

'What dost reckon ud happen to Joe's hoss if he gen him six gallons of petrol, Fred? Dost reckon he ud go any faster, 'cause you got to stand behind a tree when he's working to see whether he's moving.'

Jim and Sammy came by in their horse and float just then, just in time to hear the end of the tale.

'Taking the rise out of the War Ag., are ya?' Sammy said in his squeaky voice. 'It's not funny, you know, it's got to be paid for and it will take years to pay for their blunders.'

'What's six gallons of petrol?' I answered, 'All that will do is that it may take Joe to London and back in his car with another load of canary seed.'

'Listen, they be trying to hush it up, mind, but there bin a hellish mistake at the railway station.'

'Oh,' I said. 'Who by?'

'Some Conchies as works for the Committee, not the War Ag.,' Eric said. 'Now, again, these chaps from the town, I suppose, be entitled to their beliefs and don't agree with fighting, so the War Ag. employs um—bank clerks, counter jumpers. Some are religious.'

I nodded.

'Oh, they works all right,' Jim butted in. 'But they fetched ten tons of cement out of a truck at Ayshon Station and sowed it on Cedric's land thinking it was basic slag. The slag was in the next truck.'

Skemer grinned but admitted that both came in hundred-weight paper bags, but the slag was a darker colour.

'Don't say nothing, mind, Fred,' Jim implored. ''Cos George Pitcher at the station bin given a quid to keep it quiet.'

Henry Fanshaw had been offered the slag to clear the matter up, he knew nothing about the cement.

''Tis all fair in love and war,' Jim added.

I was really worried when Sammy talked confidentially with me about the possibility of State Farms after the war 'when they won't want the little farmers nor want their produce'.

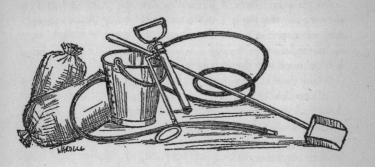

4

A.R.P. and Firewatchers

SOON AFTER WAR WAS DECLARED A MEETING WAS HELD in the school to plan for any possible air raids or gas attacks.

The chairman of the parish council was in the chair of the public meeting. We were addressed by some specialist in A.R.P. The local policeman attended.

Ex-Corporal Rose came in late and full of cider from the Apple Tree pub. He had often told us how he had been General Allenby's personal bodyguard in the '14 War. His life had been a mixture of army service and the work of a county cricket groundsman until he came to our village. Here he did odd jobs as a gardener, finding a lodging place in a stable where, as the locals called it, 'he lay rough'. Quite a few old soldiers came to this pass. No-one ever asked questions as they drummed up their tea in billycans and lived a life not unlike the privations on the Somme. But there was the difference that being in the country-side was peaceful. Cider was cheap. No, there is nothing new about the hippy.

'I propose the children keep their gasmasks in the school,' Corporal Rose shouted from his standing position at the back.

'It's the law of the land,' our chairman said, 'that they carry them backwards and forwards from home every day.'

'As General Allenby's bodyguard, I insist they are left in the school.'

'Will you please to be quiet, corporal,' the answer came from the chair.

Corporal Rose repeated his demand over and over, egged on by a few cider drinkers from the Apple Tree.

'Will you please leave the room,' the chairman insisted, 'so that we can get on with the business.'

P.C. Wood led the swearing ex-serviceman from the room.

An Air Raid Warden was appointed, Howard Cambridge, a meticulous head of our Air Raid Precautions. He formed a squad of wardens and the rota provided that in each squad one man was on the phone.

Our village had no proper mains water supply and we were issued with a hand pump and hose to draw water from the brook. We had a canvas tank which I was detailed to put on my lorry and some canvas buckets, a pickaxe, crowbar and a wheelbarrow.

Now Charles Stephenson who worked at Partridge Farm was one of the Wardens, but he said he had read in the daily paper that 'water was no good to put out an unsanitary bomb'.

'Incendiary, you myns,' Walt Gillet said, 'but you be right, it's sand bags they uses in Brummigum.'

Sammy Bosworth was appointed deputy warden. When the siren went it took his wife about five minutes to get his boots on, his feet had swollen in his slippers by the fire.

The meeting at the school had started some sort of organisation, but Mr. Cambridge's rota was always having to be amended when some young Ashton chap was called to join the forces.

So here we were amidst the orchards and the corn sheltered by Bredon Hill, thirty-six miles from Birmingham and Coventry with no military targets to speak of, just the branch railway line where eleven trains each day took passengers from our little station to any of the twenty-two stations towards Birmingham, and to the west the other way. It's true the red glow of the labouring goods trains loaded with armaments did use our branch, avoiding heavy traffic of the main line.

Fortunate, you may say; that's an understatement. It seemed to me we lived almost in a little Switzerland, and the great chugging planes at night just passed us by like birds passing a fallow field.

When the siren went Mr. Cambridge rang me, and I cycled up the road and called for Sammy Bosworth who, as I have said, had trouble putting on his boots. Then Bert Amos came and sixteen-year-old Eric Packer who worked for me.

We walked leisurely up and down the village street. Henry Fanshaw joined us dressed in his well-cut breeches and carrying a dimmed torch.

'The moon's arising over Broadway and it will soon be light enough to read a paper,' Sammy said as he nosed his way into a nearby garden and peered up at the apples on the tree by the back door.

'Time Will Richardson picked his Worcester Pearmain apples.'

'I don't think he's got much heart to bother now his brother Cedric is dead,' I said.

We looked at the rising moon as Bert Amos whispered:

'Sad job that, if only the War Ag. had left him alone, 'cos it is a quagmire in those meadows.'

We were joined by Jim Hicks who limped across the road in a pair of leather slippers.

'I yerd the hooter at Asum. A warning, unt it?'

'Yes,' I said, 'the searchlights are patterning the sky.'

'We beant worth a bomb yer,' Jim said. 'They be hellishly expensive to make.'

Sammy walked a bit further down the road asking Jim's opinion of wheat growing on Richardson's land.

'It ant got any more chance to survive the winter floods than a snowball as got in Hell.' That was final.

Near the Apple Tree pub Skemer Hill was showing a little light under the curtains. Walking up the path Sammy knelt under the window.

Eric Packer nudged me and whispered, 'Skemer's coming out through the side door, Sammy hasn't heard him.'

'What the hell do you think you be at then, Sammy, peeping through my window?'

Skemer was more than angry because he knew how nosey Sammy could be.

'Looking at your blackout, Master Hill. There are chinks of light coming through and the planes are over. You will have to blackout better than that.'

Skemer drew himself up to his full six foot and shouted for all of us to hear:

'Get off down that path afore I gives ya a smack aside the yud, and if I was thirty years younger I'd knock you ass over yud.'

'Not very pleasant at times,' Sammy muttered as he made for the gate and we laughed out in the road.

These nights with Sammy were a memory not to forget. That moonlight night, in fact, he was in my brother's yard counting the boxes of apples on the trailers ready for market: this was Sammy all over—just plain nosey.

It seemed to me that little Mr. Bosworth (for little he was) was a sort of parish constable of Victorian times.

A row of incendiary bombs dropped along the railway line a mile away and Jim Hicks shouted, 'Look up for a rattle now.'

Soon the All Clear could be heard at Evesham.

Jim Hicks and Eric Packer went home, but Sammy and I had

to report to A.R.P. headquarters and drink a cup of coffee with Mr. Cambridge till he had the All Clear what Sammy called 'official like' on the phone.

Some nights after when Coventry was bombed Sammy and I, with Eric Packer and Bert Amos, walked up the lane towards the hill and watched the flashes and saw the red glow of fire in the sky. We saw fire engines on the main road from Cheltenham heading north to the Midlands.

George Pitcher who worked on the railway was at the top of the village street. He was almost in tears as he described the fate of the women and the 'little uns' left in the cities.

'It's pitiful, you know, 'cos the war unt their affair.'

We walked silently down the road, the planes went *wow wow wow* overhead after they had unloaded.

All at once a scream like ten thousand rockets came through the wood as a plane released a bomb which fell harmlessly in a pond in the next village.

'Old Hitler done a good job last night,' Jim told me. 'Cleaned a pond out as clean as a whistle, that un ud a done more damage to Coventry.'

As more men went in the forces and the Local Defence Volunteers or Home Guard as it was called later, Mr. Cambridge recruited more fire watchers and wardens.

Charles Stephenson joined us and one week in May we were out every night and most of the night, all too conscious of the fact that we were fortunate to be working in such a pleasant place, away from the destruction of Hitler's planes. No danger of our being trapped in city streets in the middle of an inferno circled by incendiary bombs, then high explosives.

I find it interesting to look back on the night life of a village at war. It's strange considering that before 1939 the majority of our village folk would be in bed by 9.30, how people under Mr. Cambridge adapted themselves to this different time table.

Who would have thought of the W.I. for instance turning out, scurrying off down past our house to the Recreation Room when the warning went. They had a casualty station there with no casualties.

The fact remains that the kettle was boiled, the first-aid kit put out on the trestle table in the small hours of those mornings.

Let no one minimise the efficiency of these women, though it's true that all that happened was that we drank the tea and put the first-aid kit away when the All Clear sounded.

There was a sense of urgency though when mistakes did happen. Some A.R.P. smiled, some swore when an over-anxious W.I. member switched on the light in our recreation room before drawing the blackout curtains.

'They be lit up like the Crystal Palace and henemy planes overyud.'

'Damn the W.I.,' Charles Stephenson said. 'They have given away our position.'

The planes passed to their targets in the big cities and Jim Hicks said once more, 'We beunt worth a bomb, I tell ya one a them contraptions costs more money than the whole of our parish's worth.'

One night a lone plane crossed the Vale, no air-raid warning had sounded. Ashton lay sleeping.

The scream came as the bomb fell. The siren went and we met in the village street, a little man passed us running in his slippers. He ran to the houses of a widow and a spinster. It was Bill Brown who worked at Partridge Farm. Bill who had settled here from the Black Country years ago but still spoke in their dialect.

'Be yaw awright, Mrs. Blackford, and be yaw awright, Mrs. Banuhell?' Bill ran past again, then saw us and turned back.

'Always keep yawrself unda sum cuva. In a raid, I got blowed from a waggin when the Zepps bombed hower stayshun during the fust lot.'

Morning came. The bomb had dropped away from the village in a flooded wheat field belonging to Bill Richardson; blue clay was heaped in a circle around the hole. Jim Hicks' comment was, 'That cost old Hitler a few quid and look at that blue clay — we could start a brickyard here, that clay ud make some smartish bricks.'

In the Apple Tree pub that night Walt Gillet came trembling in after a day on the hill working for Mr. Bennet.

'Thee has got the shakes, Walt,' Jim said. 'How much cider of our gaffer's have you drunk out of that twelve-month-old barrel that I tapped? I know Sammy had given you permission to have a tot or two when you passed our place.'

Walt gripped a mug of cider from the Apple Tree bar and took a gulp before he spoke.

'Did ya hear that ironwork scream over last night? Now you know what Churchill meant on Sunday about keeping up our morals.'

'What about it?' the landlord said.

Walt wiped his mouth on his sleeve and said, 'One more night like last night and all my morals ull be gone.'

Wilf Richardson laughed and said, 'That's judgment on the War Ag. for taking my brother's land.'

Henry Fanshaw surprised the company when he said that by instinct he sprang across the double bed on top of his wife Flick when he heard the bomb falling. 'I thought that if the bedroom ceiling fell I could protect her with my body so I lay on top of her while it passed over.'

Jim Hicks raised his eyebrows, turned to Charles Stephenson and whispered, 'I'll warrant he laid on her for longer than the bomb was falling.'

'More fool he,' Charles answered from his corner. 'Make hay while the sun shines, her bin a gym mistress, her's lisson, I says.' 'Mind,' he continued, 'I've known the time when there was room for another body in our bed between me and the missus, that's when we had a feow words and wasn't on speaking terms, you know what I myuns, Jim, but last night I noticed her snuggled up alongside me.'

Skemer Hill came in for just half a pint. 'That's as much as the missus ull let me have,' he said. 'Her don't like ma getting out in the night.'

'What did ya think about the bomb, Skemer?' Jim said.

'Oi, Master Cambridge bin talking to me and says the end of the world's coming, it says that in the Bible.'

'What about thee money, Skemer? Be you worried?' Charles said.

'My money's under the bed, it unt safe in the bank in the town. Some's my side and some's the missus's.'

'Do you reckon we shall win the war, Skemer,' the landlord asked as he pulled another pint of beer for Henry.

'Win! Course we shall. Thee wait till Russia starts, oi, thee wait till Russia starts.'

5

Coupons

'IT WON'T BE LONG NOW AFORE EVERYTHING THAT'S worth having ull be rationed.' Skemer Hill spoke these words as we sat on cabbage crates around a wood fire on the burra (sheltered side) of the hedge one cold spring morning eating our ten o'clock bait. Jim Hicks had walked across from Sammy's fields to join me and Eric Packer.

Jim with his bread and what he called his mousetrap ration of cheese under his thumb, butted into the conversation.

'There's one thing as they can't ration though,' he said. 'That's what we used to call playing at fathers and mothers and I dare say Old Skemer still enjoys that.'

Skemer Hill's teeth nearly fell from their loose anchorage and with his mouth full of food he blurted out, 'Never bothers me.'

'Well, dost ever feel like it?' Jim said.

Skemer choked and laughed, looking first at me then at Eric Packer.

'If ever any such thoughts enter my yud I get on my bicycle now and go hell for leather up the Station Road to my cottage and my missus.'

We laughed, knowing what a reception he would have from his wife.

Jim Hicks told us that talking of coupons and rations, it was ration cards in the first war. 'Now we be hissued with books.'

'You know that Sammy Bosworth is a Jew and doesn't eat bacon,' I reminded Jim Hicks, 'and he keeps pigs. What about his bacon ration?'

'Bless the fella, we got that job fixed, me and Will Richardson. Sammy killed a pig last week, he's in the salting lead now this minute.'

'What's happening to the bacon?' Eric Packer asked.

Jim Hicks was careful with his words, 'What I'm a-going to tell ya unt strictly legal so don't broadcast it.'

We were itching to know the truth.

'In the first place,' Jim explained, 'me and Will Richardson be letting Sammy have our cheese ration and we be farm workers and gets extra you understand.'

We nodded.

Jim continued: 'Will and me be having bacon and ham in exchange, so if you chaps or folks as can be trusted be willing to part with that rubbery tack called processed cheese from America, Sammy ull exchange good home cured bacon for it.'

'I shall have to ask the missus afore I does anything as unt above board,' Skemer replied.

'Come on, you chaps, that half past ten train has gone,' Tom Wheatcroft called from the other side of the hedge.

Tom came towards the fire. 'What's the argument?' he said.

'Dost want some black-market bacon?' Jim asked him.

'No,' Tom replied, 'I got my own bacon in salt now.'

'Skemer's a bit wary about swopping his cheese ration for some of Sammy's bacon,' I said.

'I should have to ask the missus first,' Skemer muttered again.

Tom cleared his throat and said, 'Skemer, what about you and your missus flogging all your clothing coupons then?'

Skemer Hill sucked his breath. 'How did you know, Tom?'

'I haven't told a soul. 'Tis all the talk in the pub and you did brag going to Church on Sunday that you was wearing the same suit you were married in fifty years ago.'

Skemer was worried but couldn't deny he had sold his clothing coupons.

'Who would have thought of a Black Market here?' Tom said. 'Still, I thought the Hills have bought pretty well of clothes at Chapel rummage sales.'

We went on planting the spring corn, Tom and I, and Eric followed with the harrows while Skemer cut back an overgrown hedge.

So life went on in the village where things were scarce and clothes on coupons. Flour bags made good towels and table cloths and the village women had kept back some cotton bags in which the peas had been marketed the previous summer. They used them for towels and napkins for the babies.

Oh yes, and several girls married their soldier bridegrooms, smartly dressed in white silk from R.A.F. parachutes.

*   *   *

Our near neighbours at Kemerton formed a Pig Club in the 1880s. Dumbleton had a club, but we in Ashton when war came had no such a group of pig keepers.

It's always good to glance back at the origin of village affairs.

Kemerton had a book of rules printed. Members paid so much for each pig to be insured, the whole affair was done on a business footing under the Friendly Society's control.

Pig Clubs were for the benefit of cottagers who kept one or two pigs which were marked in one ear by an official of the committee, so that they could be identified. Kemerton's rules were strict; no higgler or jobber in pigs could join the club. These men were dealers at the market and could easily spread disease.

No smoking or drinking of alcohol at the club meeting, and if a member turned up under the influence of drink he was fined.

So then the Pig Clubs became a protection for the cottager. In the event of a pig being ill the member must report to the committee. The sub-committee or inspectors of pigs would decide if the vet should be called in.

If the pig died the local butcher and another member would then decide on its estimated weight. The weight was determined in scores of pounds, such as seven score or ten score. Market price was paid to the member from the funds to enable him to buy another replacement.

The various causes of death recorded in the minute book does suggest that pigs' ailments are similar to our own. For instance, a pig has a similar digestive system to ours. Inflammation of the stomach, pleurisy, pneumonia and measles were common causes of death.

So like our neighbours in nearby villages we started a Pig Club. The main reason was not to insure against the death of a pig but ensure a regular supply of rations.

The law was that by surrendering the family bacon coupons, rations known as balancer meal were issued by coupons to enable anyone to keep a pig for their own use.

One evening in April a meeting was held at our recreation room and a Pig Club was formed. Being war time the rules were simple. The local baker agreed to stock the balancer meal, a scheme for insurance was drawn up.

Sammy Bosworth was there, and I remember he asked the committee if we could get the grub cheaper. No-one, not the meanest in the room, was interested in his question.

Sammy however did provide a sort of village piggy bank where weaners or pigs of eight weeks old could be bought for about four pound apiece.

The following week every member who had not a pigsty, and there were many in this fix, was busy sticking withy posts into the garden soil and hammering corrugated iron to improvise roofs for pigsties.

Bylaws were waived aside, the ruling of so many yards of a house was ignored.

Pigs were snorting from almost every garden.

How much we all learnt from the old folk then; the folk who had kept pigs forty years before were valuable in the club with their advice. It was always said that two pigs together in one sty thrived better than one alone. Besides the company, and pigs do like company, it caused competition at feeding time, when one pig tried to outdo the other at the trough. The Ministry agreed that two members of the club could keep their pigs together in one sty and share the cost of the food and share the work. Some did just that.

The balancer meal was issued monthly. It was a small ration but enough if used wisely to mix with the swill or scraps from the household.

Instead of a dustbin being used by the back door of the houses the hogshead barrel came once more into its own. Some had smaller barrels of sixty gallons, but the wash tub as we knew it had returned. In our immediate area no-one ever referred to pig swill, it's a term used more in urban districts. We called the waste from the garden and kitchen which fermented outside the door in the barrels 'pig wash'.

So in the war our gardens were planted not only to feed ourselves but feed that creature which, when fattened, killed and salted made the most valuable pictures as flitches of bacon which hung on the kitchen walls. Jim Hicks planted a patch of parsnips in his garden to cook in the washhouse copper with the small or pig potatoes to feed his pig.

The folk I met with always told me that in the olden days the accent was on foraging or gleaning everything which could be used as food for the house. Once more the acorns from the oak trees were put in sacks to supplement the ration, the pig wash from the barrel.

'You can eat all of a pig bar the squeal,' Skemer said, and to everyone's surprise Skemer had a pig, but like its owner it was described by Sammy as one of Pharaoh's lean kind.

'More mealtimes than meals, they bwoth gets,' Charles Stephenson said.

The aroma from the pig tub was difficult to explain; some barrels had a stranger stink than others. It depended on what went in the water, from boiled cabbages mixed with cooked potato peelings, carrot tops, left over from stews, cooked beetroot, small raw apples fermented into a soupy liquid, which was ladled out with a handled bowl into the pig bucket. Then the cooked and mashed pig potatoes and parsnips were added to give it substance and last of all a few handfuls of balancer meal. The whole mixture was a sloppy, pudding-like food and the pigs thrived on it.

Of course the professionals gave their pigs a cow cabbage midday between meals and a shovelful of slack coal to help digestion.

When ladling out the wash from the tub, if some was spilt on the pig keeper's clothes the smell was difficult to get rid of.

Before the war some of the copper furnaces in the village had been removed, now people had home-made outdoor fireplaces which burnt wood and boiled the vegetables in forty-gallon steel drums.

'Skemer's feeding his pig mainly on cooked parsnips and he's too mean to buy the ration,' Walt Gillet said at the Apple Tree.

'Oi, and mark my words,' old Jim Hicks remarked, 'it ull take a good knife to cut the bacon. Parsnips make the sward [rind] devilish hard.'

Ralph Simms chuckled. He never spoke often, but now he recalled a pig that Laughing Tom killed years back when the bacon was so thin you could see through the flitches, 'Mind,' he said, 'That was old Jobey's fault, him as his up in the churchyard. Jobey wanted as much meat as possible cut from the inside spare ribs [griskins] and you can't have it both ways, you either leaves the bacon on the flitch or eats the pig meat fresh.'

Ashton was, as the old folk said, gleaning. Even the roadman was followed as he cut his swath on the verges. The pig keepers sacked the cut vetches and clover which fell from his scythe blade.

At threshing time it was no trouble to get help to keep the hungry threshing machine working at full pressure. The little master men with smallholdings came and asked me and Henry Fanshaw, yes, and Sammy, if they could have some split beans or tail or broken barley in part payment.

Pigs were so important to the household; everything possible was grist to the mill, or should I say the pig-wash tub. As the leaves fell in October and the pigs grew fat and fit to kill, our local pig butchers sharpened their knives.

A man in this trade is usually a self-employed small-holder or retired farmer. He carries his tools in a large knapsack. It was necessary in war time for him to be licensed as the pig-killing licences issued by the Ministry of Food were signed by him. We had a choice. There was Stodge who cycled from a nearby village, short and strong, quick at his job. A click from the humane killer and the pig was stuck with his butcher's knife as it lay in painless bliss on the bench.

The squeal only happened when the pig was led from its sty.

But if you weren't in a hurry, Laughing Tom was your man. For a very reasonable charge he would dispatch a pig in a professional manner, he was quick on the job once he got started, but it was important to listen to his memories of elephant-size animals which had fallen to his knife in the past, long before humane killer.

Joe Wheatcroft from Westmandcote lived in a cottage three-quarters of the way up Bredon Hill. He had killed pigs long before I was born. 'Only been around these parts,' he told me, 'since about 1900 when I came as under keeper for the General.'

The 1914 War seemed recent to him and as for the Boer War, the memory of it was clear in his mind.

Joe had to be fetched to our village by car. Short and nimble, as bald as a coot with an eye like a hawk, Joe's sense of humour, his sense of values are with him as he still hobbles around. We hope he sees a hundred years around the countryside which has been a part of him for well over ninety.

It was usual for several villagers to engage Joe for the day when he would kill about four pigs belonging to the club. Somehow over the years he had developed a knack of coaxing his prey to the bench without any fuss or noise.

''Tis use,' he told me as he talked nicely, leading the pig from the sty to the pig bench.

Jim Hicks had a fourteen-score animal fit for the butcher and arranged with Bert Amos, Charles Stephenson and Walt Gillet to have their four pigs 'put down' as he called it by Joe on the same day.

The licences were issued, Henry Fanshaw had agreed to fetch Joe over with Thomas Bennet's pony and governess cart. The straw boltens were taken to the four styes at Partridge Farm. Jim had taken a few hours off work at Sammy's to help in the joint affair.

He arrived at the styes at dawn and to his dismay and disappointment his pig was not fit to kill. Almost in tears I met him in the village street.

'Yur's me licence,' he said to me, 'but me pig can't be killed today, her's on a brimming.' I knew what he meant: a gilt or young sow in season.

I said, 'That's a pity, but will it matter?'

'Now look yur, Master Fred,' he said, 'you know damn well it will matter. The bacon won't take the salt, it's been proved without doubt that sows in season won't take the salt, they just go bad. Another thing, it's the same with women.' I looked at Jim giving him the impression that this was news to me, but I had heard it all before.

'Women,' he said, 'as be suffering from their monthly must never touch bacon as it lies salting in the salting trough. Years ago when I was but a bwoy chap, a pig went wrong in the salt at Beckford, just because a young servant girl had touched the flitches when her wasn't well, so to speak.'

I nodded. 'Sorry, Jim, what will you do?'

'Well her's be all right in a day or two, but the licence is for today and you knows how particular they be at the Ministry and I can't afford to use this licence when it might mean me going up the steps at the Petty Sessions.'

'Won't they alter the date at the Food Office?' I asked.

'Oi,' he replied, 'but that myuns a journey to Asumm.'

'I'm going to the market with a few nets of sprouts. Will you come with me?' This offer of mine Jim accepted and at ten o'clock after we had had a cup of cocoa together at my place and Jim had put on his best jacket and his light shoes we started.

Jim got out at the Town Hall and I went on to the market.

'I'll pick you up at half past eleven outside the Town Hall,' I told him.

He was there looking agitated holding a piece of paper in his hand as I arrived with my Austin 10 tourer.

'Everything all right, Jim? Have you got the date altered?' I said.

'Oi, after a smartish argument. Women,' he added, 'they don't understand. I told the one at the Food Office that my sow was on a brimming and her looked at me sort a vacant, then her fetched another woman a bit older, the one as issued the licence I suppose. "Now, Mr. Hicks," said she. "I don't understand why you can't have that pig of yours killed today." Of course that meant me having to tell her about sows in season not taking the salt and they thought I was pulling their leg so I told them straight that women had no business to touch meat either.'

'You didn't,' I said.

'As true as God made little apples I told them the story of the Beckford wench and they both went into another office a laughing thur heads off, but they altered the date to next Thursday.'

We arrived home but as Jim got out of my car, he said, 'These yur officials as makes these licences have got to be paid. For all the years I've kept pigs there has never been this trouble.'

Jim sighed, looked again at his licence and said, 'Of course the townies will never know like thee and me the ways of dumb animals.'

We both went to dinner.

Dinner in our villages has always been at one o'clock among the farming folk. The market gardeners of Evesham of the old school took theirs at twelve o'clock.

While I ate the boiled bacon with the potatoes and sprouts my mind went back once more, this time to Charles Lamb and the fable of the origin of the roast pig. The story is simple and believable.

Bo Bo the Chinese boy played with fire which reduced the poor thatched makeshift cottage to ashes. His father was gathering beech mast to feed his sow who some days before had farrowed a litter of nine, all of which died in the fire, which spread to the primitive sty.

To quote Lamb: 'While he was thinking what he should say to his father, and wringing his hands over the smoking remnants of one of those untimely sufferers, an odour assailed his nostrils, unlike any scent which he had before experienced. What could it proceed from?—not from the burnt cottage—he had smelt that smell before. . . . He next stooped down to feel the pig, if there were any signs of life in it. He burnt his fingers, and to cool them he applied them in his booby fashion to his mouth. Some of the crumbs of the scorched skin had come away with his fingers, and for the first time in his life (in the world's life indeed, for before him no man had known it) he tasted—*crackling*!'

The roast pig was so delicious that when his father arrived

home in a rage, Bo Bo was still eating a new food, not raw sucking pig but roasted meat.

So I thought that here in the 1940s, thousands of years since Bo Bo, I was eating pig meat cooked, and with the shortage of butcher's meat it was precious food. No doubt Jim was still thinking of the foolish woman at the Food Office.

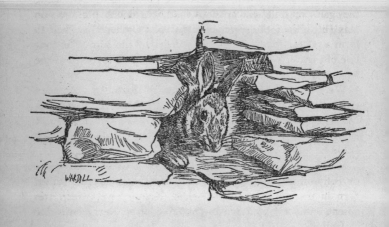

6

Voices That Were Gone

IT'S TRUE TO SAY THAT ANY HILL LIKE BREDON HILL,
a thousand feet above sea level with vales and valleys all around,
has been a stronghold for our ancestors. Here was a refuge from
the danger of both foe and flood.

For such hills in the last war things had changed. I suppose that
if the threatened invasion of these islands had come they might
have been a bastion for defence, but here on Bredon Hill it was
a kind of macabre grandstand where the not too distant ravages
of the bombed Midland places could be seen and heard.

I walked the hill by day where the sky above was like a race-
course paddock. The 'planes took off from the circle of 'dromes

and manœuvred and jockeyed themselves into formations like horses before a race. In the battle above Birmingham and Coventry the tactics of defence were rehearsed over the hill.

Thoughts on a hillside walk seem to elevate as the land rises; they gain depth and reality. On a clear day the clump of trees on May Hill beyond the tower of Gloucester Cathedral seemed to form a companionship with our beeches by the barn. The long line of the Cotswold edge was nearer, but this elevation was the beginning of the Limestone Country.

We were so small, our hill lying as it does like a stranded whale between the Cotswold Edge and the Malverns. Nevertheless the track where the Roman pack animals carried the salt along one of the Saltways near the smaller Dumbleton Hill could be followed.

So as I walked away from the Cotswold side towards the Tower or Folly on the Hill Top, I passed the beeches and the ruined barn in my search of a sandy-faced Radnor ewe, which was absent without leave from my hundred or so Kerry ewes due to lamb.

Basking in the February sunshine she stood in the Parish Quarry where two strong lambs sucked and bunted at her udder. She whipped her head towards me like a startled deer, then carried on foraging among the wild thyme and trefoil on the quarry bank.

Why come up here to lamb, I thought, far away from the feeding troughs and hay racks in the Vale?

I whistled and she and her nimble lambs ran towards the bridle gate. Opening it I let them through and watched them as they made their way to the flock down below.

Skipper, my collie dog, was trying to dislodge some stone from a boundary wall, he whined as he wore his nails down against the tightly packed stone.

'Wait, boy, let me help you. We can do with a rabbit for dinner this week.'

Carefully taking away the stone in the wall revealed Skipper's quarry with its ears laid, its back towards us, fearing the worst.

It was little trouble to put my hand under its back legs and pull it from its hiding place and kill it, just making one less of the hordes of its kind among the stony fields.

After replacing the stones into the wall I took a walk to the Iron Age camp near the Tower. The entrenchments here, monuments to our primitive ancestors, remained the same as when I first saw them as a boy. Maybe in a thousand years little will have changed.

Looking back across the Vale to the green roads, the Portways and Saltways of the Cotswolds were further evidence of monuments in the history of primitive man. I remembered the human skeleton that Dad and Cousin Tom had unearthed in a field below, bones of ancient days. The hill was oozing with history. The green little copper coins of the Romans lay plain to see among the rows of winter oats on sunny mornings after a wet night.

Just how many years had passed since the great battle between the men of the Wicce and the invaders. How many lay sleeping under my feet from wars so different from the hail of incendiary and high explosive bombs showered on our cities?

As the 'planes took off from Defford 'drome the sheep on the hill and the rabbits at their burrows ignored the whirr of their propellers when they dipped low overhead.

The runways at Defford looked like a concrete desert and surely would not remain like the earthworks dug by early man on the hill. How many brave hearts lie sleeping here and for what was the blood spilt so freely? This was a question which has never been answered.

Wollas Hall lay in a combe below, a place of history. It was supposed to have given shelter to some of the Gunpowder plotters. Was the fifth of November going to be celebrated once more when the peace came?

What a place to be, I thought, midway between Gloucester and Worcester; it was so easy to contemplate alone on the men who had lived on the hill, where their voices had rung out through the wooded plateau, and to kick aside the fossilised fish in the quarry and think back millions of years before when water covered this part of the scene.

I thought, what was eternal? The camp was age-old but eternal things were the sun and the moon which at one time shone on a different scene.

Between Gloucester and Worcester, I thought again, yes, between Cromwell and the King, and looking towards Elmley I saw the bended road where a Mr. Moore pulled his loaded hay wagon in front of Cromwell's troops and hindered him from pursuing the King, and so below lay Moore's Farm, given to Mr. Moore for his help to Charles.

Turning back as the sun lowered over the Malverns, Will Richardson walked up to me. He came under the wall walking briskly, remarking to me the beauty of the sunset.

'You're late, aren't you, Will?' I said.

Will turned, looking through his field-glasses, and told me that this was his usual time to climb the hill. 'Twilight is the best time to see the beauty of nature.'

I agreed and asked him what he could see.

'Down Severn Valley they have painted the gasholder green by Gloucester Cathedral. It won't be dark for another hour but it will be moonlight and the German 'planes may be over again tonight.'

I nodded.

'This is where your father and Mr. Bailey used to build the sainfoin rick,' Will said.

Pausing a bit and looking at the ruined barn, I remembered the faces of the men who were gone. Wet-eyed, I thought of Jack Hunting who, with me, caught four rabbits in four wires by the bridle gate.

'Do I see a tear?' Will asked me as we stood silently on what to me was almost holy ground.

'Maybe, Will, but it's so easy to picture the track where I led the horse that worked the elevator pole when we built the rick. You remember Jack's walk, how he stooped, and how upright the shepherd stood.'

'Yes, and the snow which filled the gully when I helped you and Tom Wheatcroft to fodder the heifers in a howling blizzard.'

'You remember faces then, Will?' I said.

'Yes, the faces that are gone, my poor brother who lost what I call his birthright, when he was dispossessed of his land.'

We agreed that the local committee men were on Cedric's side against the War Ag.

We spoke of the menace of the aeroplanes and I thought of my cousin Jim who never came back in the Wellington bomber from over Germany.

'I expect you are like me, Will. When some son of Ashton is going and he shakes my hand I wonder, is this our last farewell?'

'Yes,' Will said, 'and I often hear Cedric's voice calling the cows where the wheat land flooded.'

'Look, Will, let's not be too glum. See how the patchwork quilt of the land has changed. If the land was left to nature alone it would be a jungle or a swamp. See the rows of green wheat and the leafless hedges. We shall need these crops now the German submarines and 'planes are attacking our convoys of food from other countries.'

Will took from his pocket a silver-banded pipe and lit it. The glow was more distinct as the light was getting dim. We stood between sunset and moonrise on a hill so quiet apart from the distant bleat of a ewe and the plaintive call of her lamb. The starlings passed over like a swarm of bees on the way to the chattering roost of Hinton Roughs.

The searchlights on the Cotswolds were focusing their beams as the first early 'planes came over.

'Reconnaissing,' I said. 'Geoff was home last week,' I recalled. 'He's a smart chap, in the Medical Corps, you know.'

'At least he doesn't have to kill then,' Will replied. 'This was your Sunday walk up here, wasn't it?'

I looked again at the rickyard by the barn and saw Geoff ploughing the light soil with two horses. I felt sad that the young men were leaving us from the fields.

Jack Lambley came to mind, hoeing sprouts at so much a row

in the next field. I saw the yellow charlock fall beneath his hoe blade and recalled the chats under the wall at dinner-time with him and Jim and Uncle George.

The faces that were gone.

Uncle George and the peapickers—it was all like a dream.

'I'll be on my way home now, Will, are you coming?' I said.

Will laughed. 'What, now, just as the moon rises over the Broadway Hill? Not likely, this is all I've left now, the solitude of Bredon. Many a night I've slept up here under the stars in summer. Yes, Fred, when you sleep under the stars with just a mackintosh between you and the dewy grass, then you must acknowledge the power of the Almighty.'

7

The Defenders of Ashton

WHEN THE FIRST LOCAL DEFENCE VOLUNTEERS WERE
formed to keep watch and stem a possible invasion, countrymen
in the main had certain advantages over the townsmen. A
villager who has been used to stalking rabbits and pigeons with
his shot gun uses the natural lie of the land to hide from the
animals and birds, he cowers down, bent low beside the high
hedge or stone wall, his dress is less showy than that of his
friends in the town.

Against these inbred qualities it must be said that the town
dweller is better material to mould into a smart and upright

soldier who will march and not take the long strides of the men who have followed the plough and ambled after the full uddered milking cows up a country lane on a warm summer's afternoon.

So Colonel Somerton, ex-Cavalry Officer, marshalled his men. Never before had he as an officer had such a mixed company to school.

The Colonel had been with some of the army's cream and here he was, as he said himself, four years on trespass down here at seventy-four years old, given this task. He picked his officers from ex-servicemen of the First War. The men mounted guard at the Cuckoo Pen, a plateau on the hill where a shed was erected near the beech trees.

'You chaps have enough twelve-bore shot guns among you and cartridges for a dawn and dusk watch on the hill. Look for anything suspicious. Jerry may invade, who knows?' he said.

The beginning of this little army was so simple as men volunteered to keep watch over our village.

At this stage no drill had been practised, there were just two men with twelve-bore guns, walking as the dawn broke and waiting, writing notes in the book, describing what they had seen from the shed on the hill.

Again at dusk two more men were armed at the Cuckoo Pen.

On a hill where the rabbits ate everything green in a dry summer and the farmers, farm workers, small-holders shot every Saturday in winter, sending hampers of fresh-killed rabbits to Birmingham and elsewhere, our men were quick on the draw or on the trigger. It's a fact of life to the shooting men and death to the rabbit that a hundred shots of lead to reach this fast little animal on the run must be placed straight and in an instant.

I have a great admiration for the unassuming countryman who walked casually with his double-barrelled twelve-bore. Many of the guns in the '40s were hammer guns and how often have I seen him on these Saturdays cock the hammers back silently in a way he and I knew when the terrier dogs were drawing a blackberry bush, where a startled rabbit would bolt in a direction which was anyone's guess.

The potential Home Guards rarely missed, so there was some comfort that in the face of an enemy their shots would be on target.

Yes, human life is sacred, but so is survival.

Skemer Hill was drafted into the Home Guard with Bert Amos, Mr. Bennet's foreman, who worked under Henry Fanshaw, but Henry, who was on the 'phone, stayed as an Air Raid Warden with Mr. Cambridge and myself.

Skemer was going on guard duty to the Cuckoo Pen as dusk fell late one summer's evening; his path was through the Close Orchard and over the stile at the top end. The rota that week paired Skemer with Corporal Baker, a smart younger chap who kept to the rule book. He challenged Skemer at the stile where he awaited his companion for the evening's watch.

'Halt, who goes there?' Corporal Alec Baker called as the shadowy figure of Skemer emerged from beneath the laden branches where the Conference pears almost touched the turf.

Skemer made no answer, but just puffed his way short breathed up the hill. At sixty-nine he told me that he was not the man he was forty years ago.

Alec levelled his twelve-bore at the old chap.

'Halt or I fire,' he called. This practical joke, if joke it was, was too much for Skemer who replied:

'Don't be so damn silly, Alec, thee knowst very well who I be, and besides it's an offence to point a gun at anybody.'

'Everything's fair in love and war,' Alec told him.

'Have you been in love, Skemer?'

'Bless the fella, years ago I done some sweet-hearting on this yer hill after Chapel.'

Skemer then told Alec as they kept watch over our parish how he once courted a girl named Jenny the Gem.

'Dost know how her served me one summer's night?' he asked Alec. 'After Chapel we walked right to the top of this yer hill, then her said "I don't wish to keep company with you any more".'

Skemer told me next day how the corporal had threatened to shoot him and about Jenny.

I said, 'Well, why did she give you up?'

Skemer laughed. 'Oi, I wasn't forrad enough for her. Her was going out with Herbert who had been to the Boer War. Dost know what her told me?' Skemer said in a whisper as we stood out of earshot under the hedge. 'Her told ma as Herbert put his hand on her knee and she didn't know what his intentions were. I knowed though,' he added, 'and it don't take much thinking over.'

Then I persuaded Skemer to tell me how he married Nellie.

'Oi, on the rebound so to speak, I'd courted her sister Agnes for twelve months, then her chucked me up after the banns had been read. We'd bin asked in Church twice, within six months I married Nellie, and Jim Hicks' brother along of some of the other chaps at the Manor Farm said as we was obliged to get married.'

'Obliged, why?' I said.

'Oi done the last job first and that Nellie was in the family way.'

I nodded, 'Well, was she?'

'Two years to the day when the first youngster arrived, and our gaffer said, "You have been a good while making that one." Of course I knowed different, I knowed it was a leg pull.'

It was fortunate for me that Skemer had to be on guard on the hill about once a week when his turn came, fortunate too that the other men who carried the gun were better shots than Skemer. Jim Hicks said that he would not have hit a barn if he had been inside it. No marksman or rabbiter, a man much better with a hoe among the swedes and turnips than shooting, but Skemer did make history one Sunday afternoon as the companies from our district lined up in Evesham outside the Bon-Marché, or what Skemer called The Bran Mash.

They were to be inspected by a high-ranking officer from Worcester.

'This yer General,' Jim Hicks said, 'has got more letters after his name than the number of pigs in a fair-sized litter.'

The men were tired of waiting for the late arrival of the Staff car from Worcester carrying the old General.

'Stand at ease,' Lieutenant Cowley ordered his men as he walked up and down his uneven squad.

Skemer Hill lit his pipe, others had a drag at a Woodbine.

'Attention,' Lieutenant Cowley called as the Staff car pulled up and the General marched towards the men.

In a flash Skemer pushed his pipe, still alight, into a pocket of his battledress blouse.

As the General passed the men stood as upright as their crooked spines would allow. Skemer was on fire, the smoke from the khaki clothes smelt like a rag from burning a Monday-morning copper boiler.

Colonel Somerton chose his men like a dealer choosing horses. Smart young tractor drivers who spent their winter evenings in the woods, shooting the hordes of pigeons which came to roost after packing their crops under their beaks with clover and spring cabbage, were his marksmen. These, with the ex-servicemen who had worked their small-holding between the wars, made up a company of good shots, some crack shots, potential snipers on our hill.

When cartridges were twopence each and rabbits a shilling these chaps could bowl over the driven rabbit or hare and also they shot pigeons which plagued the green crops during the day. How often have I seen them fall with such a thud to the ground from the flocks in the twilight air, sometimes bursting their full crops of food before they had a chance to perch in the tall larches, the straight ash trees of our wood.

As time went on the different Corps were formed. Sergeant Gillet was in charge of the Quartermaster's stores under a Lieutenant from World War I. It's been said that when the uniform was issued and the rifles came Sergeant Gillet proved himself in fitting the men up as well as his few sizes of clothes would allow.

The story that a pint of beer for the Sergeant at the pub would buy an extra pair of W.D. boots was never true.

So in uniform the men marched up and down our street, armed and at the ready.

Skemer was drafted into the Medical Corp with Jim Hicks, a squad where he could do little harm, and stretcher carrying for him was not unlike carrying the pot hampers of apples and pears from my orchard.

Lieutenant George Cowley, a War Ag. officer unpaid, had served with distinction in France in the 1914 War. A likeable chap, tall and lean, distinguished with a Roman nose, George had a gentlemanly manner; his ancestors had farmed Bredon Hill since time immemorial. In his younger days he would pitch the hay from the walley or windrow to the waggons all day long with nothing to eat but home-made bread and cheese and a water bottle to drink from.

No, George wasn't teetotal, he would take a drop of beer at evening time and a pipe of tobacco as he leant on one of his farm gates, and planned his work. No smoking in the rickyard for George nor for his men was the rule.

He worked in the Home Guard to a system where the men under him knew that the details were vital, he was smart when he took his men to the woods for target practice in a place where the regular Worcesters fired at the circles.

George's eye was still keen, his lead bullets made a pattern for the men to follow, George moulded his men with dignity.

H.Q. was decided upon as a district meeting place at the Dog and Muffler, a little pub off the main road, away from the convoys of green camouflage among the cherry trees at Appleton, a hamlet in the middle of Colonel Somerton's controlled area.

Here decisions were made by the officers and N.C.O.s, here petrol was allowed for cars to carry the officers to the almost nightly meetings.

P.C. Wood was helpless. P.C. Wood's ambition in life was to summons for misuse of petrol.

The Home Guard under the Colonel were a law unto themselves. The Colonel had power to call meetings. The men drank deeply from the limited supply of beer and the unlimited supply of scrumpy cider at the Dog and Muffler.

After a council of war at H.Q. Skemer Hill was dismissed from service for letting a Mills bomb roll back into a trench on Sunday after the pin had been removed. The squad scattered, no-one was hurt. Young Packer, who worked with him, joined in Skemer's place. He, like Bert Bradfield who worked a small-holding, had an eye like a hawk. Bert was good material for soldiering the hill. His ancestors had served generations before. Bert would have been a regular but for a lung condition he contracted getting wet through on the land.

Sunday morning roll call revealed a good turn-out, the Colonel said, but Lieutenant George Cowley was concerned with two who were habitual absentees.

One was a farmer who always seemed to be calving a cow. The other was Len Wilkes, who came here to drive another of Bennet's tractors.

'Wilkes,' the Lieutenant called three times without a reply.

'Where's Wilkes this morning? Amos, he's your neighbour.'

'In bed, sir,' Bert Amos replied.

'I'll bed him,' the irate Lieutenant said, half annoyed and half disappointed.

Len was a smart young chap, short and agile, but Saturday night's cider often kept him dozey under Sunday morning's bedclothes.

When Len was on parade the old Lieutenant called him out of the uneven line of the very young and very old of the villagers.

'I'm disappointed in you, Len,' he said in a fatherly way, 'I had my eye on you for promotion.'

'Sorry, sir,' came the reply from the Sunday morning sleeper. 'It won't happen again.'

Len Wilkes, who had captained the village darts teams in the local league and once was in the running for the *News of the World* championship, was on parade the next Sunday. At eight o'clock sharp an army lorry arrived, picking up the local Home

Guard Company to take them to Tyddesley Wood for firing practice.

With polished rifles our men in battle dress arrived at the Range.

'Now, Wilkes, show us your mettle,' Lieutenant Cowley called as Len lay among the sandbags ready to shoot at the circular target.

Len had spent Saturday night at the Apple Tree drinking cider and flighting his feathered arrows at the circles on the cork dart board.

So with this still in his mind, a mind fuddled by last night's cider, he aimed at the top of the circle on the target.

The leaden bullet pinged through the clearing in the wood, landing just where Len intended.

'Too high,' called George Cowley.

'Double top,' Len replied. 'Don't we have to start scoring with a double?'

Even George smiled as his men called out: 'Up in Annie's room.'

It's true Len made a respectable pattern around the bull's eye with his remaining rounds.

'Now, men,' George Cowley said seriously, 'there is the question of the Church Bells. Our orders from the War Office are that they are to be rung if there is an invasion. You, Private Amos, and you, Private Baker, are to ring those bells only on my instructions. If King Dick tells you to ring them they are not to be rung, is that quite clear?'

Jim Hicks, who had been to school with Lieutenant Cowley and worked with him on the land, just could not bring himself to address him by rank, but blurted out:

'Who the hell's King Dick, George? I have never yeard of he.'

'Enough, Hicks, you have your orders,' the Lieutenant replied.

Those Sunday mornings when the local Company marched up and down our village street were memorable. There is no doubt at all that Lieutenant Cowley and Sergeant Gillet did a good job with the recruits. Twenty years after their demob from the First War these old soldiers injected a reasonable drill into what Burns would have described as the Awkward Squad. We in the village saw an improvement in a few weeks in the formation of the men. Ex-Corporal Lofty Rose, full of arthritis, marched in his ragged civvies beside the Home Guard. He looked with critical eye from his lone path on the roadside verge.

Left, right, left, right, he muttered, and swaggered with his arms swinging. He was just trying to instil some of his former guardsman technique into our men, but it's fair comment that to make the old men off the land, who had walked in an almost nautical roll behind the plough, into marching men was as impossible as a cart horse jumping Bechers Brook to win the Grand National.

We in the village knew that Will Richardson would never join the forces who guarded our hill.

What went through that middle-aged bachelor's mind was obvious to me. His brother had been dispossessed of the two fields and cowshed known as The Butts. 'To rob us of our Birthright,' Will related to me the facts so many times.

'Poor Cedric, why couldn't they leave him alone, my only brother!' he sighed.

P.C. Woods called on Will in his usual undiplomatic way and took him a paper ordering him to join the Home Guard. Will ripped it up in front of him saying: 'Take that tunic off and I'll fight you in the road.'

The constable went away without a word, he was aware that Will when he was incensed was a man to avoid. It's true that Richardson would have done time in jail had he struck the officer but it's also true that the man in blue wasn't keen on trouble.

Will Richardson registered as a Conscientious Objector, working at times for Sammy Bosworth and most summers fruit-picking on the other side of the hill. On winter evenings he sat on an outcrop of stone just below the Cuckoo Pen where the Home Guard did their watch. He sat there with field-glasses watching the floods as they covered Cedric's meadows where the War. Ag. planted wheat.

Will was a loner, a thinker, British to the core, but unable to accept the bureaucracy which robbed Cedric and him of his little bit of independence, the last lot of land which belonged to a family who had farmed this side of the hill for six hundred years.

'Will Richardson's a spy,' Sergeant Gillet said to his officers.

'If he is a spy you know your orders,' the Colonel said.

'What's the evidence?' Colonel Somerton added.

Sergeant Gillet was hesitant, then Private Amos said that Richardson spent his summer picking apples, and he shone his torch when the enemy 'planes were over.

'Now look here, men, don't do anything damn silly such as shooting at him or such. Do what I say; anything suspicious report to me.'

The apples were plentiful at Bredons Norton. Will Richardson picked the fruit until nightfall in October; he was what is known as lissom or agile up a forty-rung ladder.

Bredons Norton to the west of our hill overlooks the bend in the River Avon as it snakes its way towards Tewkesbury. Will liked working there, he could forget the Butts and Cedric and all that those water meadows had meant to him. He worked with evacuees, refugees, Jews and folk who seemed to fit in with Will's philosophy.

Jim Hicks was not at all pleased that Will had deserted the village scene, the harvest, to work in an alien village.

'Trust him, the occud crater, to work over yonder when Sammy Bosworth's behind with his ground work.'

Will walked across the hill every morning enjoying the company of his black retriever dog, drinking in the pure air as the rabbits scurried to their burrows and the coveys of partridges took off from the springy turf like groups of fighter 'planes.

No-one knew at Bredons Norton that Will had opted out of the Home Guard. Will had been essentially a man of our village, as much a part of it as the village cross, but so few people understood the reason why he never donned the khaki on Sunday mornings.

The apples were almost harvested and as the days drew in Will walked over the hill under the stars to his home. He was tired, the nights grew cold with a touch of frost in the air.

The Home Guard kept watch at the Cuckoo Pen as the German bombers took their usual course to Birmingham and the Midlands.

It was Sergeant Gillet and Len Wilkes' turn to be on guard at the Cuckoo Pen hut that night, a hut which was on the footpath used by Will on his way home from apple picking. The searchlights criss-crossed the Vale, the 'planes carried their loads quite unconcerned, with two men in khaki and Will on the hill.

Will sat down with his dog Rosie on the outcrop of limestone below the guard post. When he lit his pipe Sergeant Gillet and young Len ran with rifles at the ready, accusing Will of giving signals to the enemy 'planes by showing a light.

Rosie snarled, Will grinned, and once more he lived his life in peace refusing to be a target for abuse from men whose fathers and grandfathers had been glad of a crust of bread from his forebears. Oh yes, his mother had sent chocolates and cigarettes to the trenches of France in 1915, she had provided the baby clothes for the Gillets and their children.

Will would not be intimidated by the uncouth; he went home when he felt like it.

Colonel Somerton gave orders the next Sunday that Richardson was to be left alone. He had made certain inquiries about him and concluded that the man was quite harmless.

Colonel Somerton decided the following summer that the plateau on Bredon Hill would be good for a mock battle.

This manœuvre was to be largely directed by old Lieutenant Cowley. The villagers in their Home Guard company were to meet on the very spot where a great slaughter took place at the Iron Age Camp in prehistoric times. The spot also was where the Whitsuntide Games were held one hundred years ago.

Here where Grandfather, the Bradfields, the Bakers, did the ancient game (if game it could be called) of shin kicking, and fought bare fisted for belts, and here where the coconut stall was wrecked by our villagers because the travelling man gave the wrong change.

Here our grandfather rolled his coconuts down the hill towards the river.

Sergeant Gillet informed the local company that a night was to be spent after the battle in La Lu Barn. Plenty to eat and drink, he said, so no need to bring rations. The Ashton men approached from the quarry. Lieutenant Cowley was a kind of umpire who declared the killed and wounded.

As Frank from Bredon moved among the leaves of a mountain ash tree Tom, an old soldier from Ashton, picked him off at a hundred yards.

'Good job Tom hadn't got live ammo in his firing piece,' Jim Hicks said, 'because I've never known him miss a sitting bird or rarely one in flight.'

Ding dong the blank cartridges marked down any of the enemy who were not under cover.

Jim Hicks slunk back to the quarry when the Bredon men advanced.

'Keep yer yuds down, you chaps,' he said. 'We shall all be as dead as mutton else.'

As the sun set and the Lieutenant congratulated his men on their stealth but not always their camouflage, the battle was declared a draw and the Ashton Company marched to the barn.

Here Sergeant Gillet was scooping out tin mugfuls of what Jim Hicks called skilly from a big pot on the fire.

'It unt bad, it tastes of inions,' Jim said. 'But what about some fittle to go along with it?'

The Sergeant then broke the news that Colonel Somerton had ordered iron rations, 'So it's one biscuit apiece, then to bed.'

Jim Hicks told me that he had seen some pandemoniums before, but not like the desertion from Bredon. Bill Brown from

Bennet's Farm led his pals down the rough road when darkness fell to the Apple Tree pub.

It snowballed as others followed. At least two men went home to their wives and were on the hill before daybreak in the morning.

The officers slept in the farm cottage near the barn. They never knew how many got away.

Arthur, an ex-Grenadier from the First War and a Corporal in the Home Guard, lay on the hay alongside of Joe, a slouching carter off the land who ploughed a straight furrow but would never be able to march. 'Too long in the tooth,' Jim said. 'He was like me, we does our best.'

Joe still had his dreams. He may have dreamt of fairy princesses or bathing belles, who knows? He snored the night away alongside Arthur. Arthur got little sleep. Then Joe slipped his one arm around Arthur's waist, then another. His bristly face met his.

Arthur could stand it no longer. Waking his companion up, Arthur shouted, 'Ay, Joe, it yunt Alice you be making up, it's me.'

Joe woke and, finding himself in a hay barn partly filled with men, he sighed and whispered, 'Damn it, I thought I was sleeping anant Alice and her was wanting me. Still, perhaps tomorrow night,' and among titters of laughter once more the few who stayed the night slept on the hay.

These exercises would have been useful had the enemy landed. Who knows, our little mob might have used their initiative and scattered the enemy. They would have done their best, I'm sure.

8

Lilies on the Land

WHEN THE WOMEN'S LAND ARMY CAME TO OUR
village, old land workers raised their eyebrows. They were
dubious of city girls tackling the hard graft of farm work. Older
women in particular thought that they and they alone were able
to hoe and weed the onions, pick the beans and strawberries and
sow fertiliser.

It's odd how, in time of crisis, young folk in particular can
adapt themselves to a completely new way of life. The young
lads on the farm were excited at the prospect of fresh young
faces in the village.

Thomas Bennet, who himself was a city man, told his Bailiff, Henry Fanshaw, to employ four girls from the hostel on the hill to work on his farm.

They arrived one Monday morning in May. Henry met them as they stood in the yard by his office, giggling at the prospect of life in the open air away from it all.

'Take these hoes to the pea field. Bert Amos will show you what to do.'

The little group walked down our village street to where the straight rows of peas were almost in blossom. Here these girls in khaki bib and brace overalls, hatless with short-sleeved shirts open at the neck and brand new Wellingtons met the village women, Flo Gillet, Sarah Brown and Annie Stephenson.

'Huh,' Annie Stephenson said, 'what sights you see when you haven't got ey gun.'

Daphne, Christine, Sally and Wendy looked at the almost Victorian picture of women in agriculture. Here they were dressed as their own mothers had been, in long skirts, buttoned up boots, black stockings. Annie still wore a cotton bonnet, the other two had straw hats weathered by sun and wind.

'It's like this yer,' Annie Stephenson spoke up to Bert. 'If these yer girls be going to have the same wages as we do, it's only right they will do as much work.'

Bert had the girls grouped around him as he took a hoe and drew the blade either side of a row of peas. The groundsel and the chickweed was cut under the ground and Bert's hoe pulled the weeds away from the peas on to the two feet of clean earth where the horse hoe had skimmed.

'That's how you do it,' he told Daphne, 'and don't forget to pull by hand the weeds you can't cut with the hoe.'

The four girls started across the field. With backs bent they worked as Bert had shown them, all the morning they lagged a little behind the village women who had hoed peas since they left school.

At dinner-time the sun warmed the earth as the girls ate their spam sandwiches and drank from their flasks under the hedge. The village women went home to their dinner, coming back at two o'clock.

'Look, Chris,' Daphne said, 'we have got to show that we can work as well as anybody. After dinner we will keep level and then pass them old Annie, Flo and Sarah.'

With aching backs and blistered hands the Land Girls hoed alongside the regulars, then led by Daphne they passed them, reaching the hedge at the end of their rows a few yards in front.

Leaning on their hoes to rest a minute until Mr. Bennet's regular workers finished their rows, the girls turned back again with renewed vigour and soon were twenty yards ahead in what appeared to be a race.

Bert Amos and Henry Fanshaw came along riding on a dray pulled by one of Bennet's Suffolk horses. Henry, we knew, was not much of a man to judge whether a job was being done properly, so he called on Bert.

'Are they hoeing these peas all right, Bert? Or are they just smothering the weeds?'

Bert scuffed the soil aside and leant down behind where the girls had hoed.

'They are making a good job of it, Henry, quite as good as Annie.'

Here another little battle was fought and won. A battle in a pea field, not between enemy forces, but between age and experience and young girls with guts and determination to prove that a good young 'un can sometimes be better than a good old 'un.

Just where did these girls come from was a question the village folk wanted to know.

The first members of the W.L.A. came to our village from Wills' tobacco factory at Bristol. Their hair, their clothes were yellow with nicotine. One was platinum blonde or peroxide blonde. Charles Stephenson declared, 'Hur yud's as black as the hace a spades when its natural.'

So when the peas were hoed and harvest began, a great drought set in. The air was hot night and day, the grass as brown as a hare's pelt. Men discarded the flannel undershirt, donned the battered panama hats among the stooks of corn.

Daphne and Christine wore a thing called a snood to keep their hair in place. They too found the heat overpowering in the field.

Bert Amos had taught them to drive two iron-wheeled Fordson tractors. Daphne drove the one pulling the corn reaper or binder while Christine used hers to pull the loads of sheaves to the rick.

Our village folk, Jim Hicks and Sammy Bosworth in particular, had never spent their summer holidays idling on some sunny beach; a day at Weston-super-Mare on a church outing was about their limit.

Daphne and Christine were determined to take the benefit of this hot summer weather. At Cheltenham one Saturday they each bought a sun top and the shortest of shorts. To make the most of the sunshine they turned up the hem of the shorts.

Bert Amos was quite proud of his two workers who bounced on the iron tractor seats which he padded with sacks of hay, and here they were, telling us all in their way that, however hard the work on the tractor, they were feminine.

Annie Stephenson was shocked at what she called the brazen hussies; but I'm sure Bert was impressed by the well-developed, only half-covered bust of Daphne.

Never in history had anything of this nature happened in our village. Charles, Walt and Bert were watched by their working wives and ordered to eat their bait or ten o'clock lunch far away from the dusty headland where the girls lay in the sun, away from the scent of Nivea cream which they rubbed on each other's skinning backs and bronzed arms.

How different on the land where the smell of twist tobacco and horses had wafted across harvest fields for generations.

'There ull soon be some bastard kids up at the hostel,' Jim Hicks told Sammy Bosworth. ''Tis more than these bwoy chaps in the village can stand. These wenches be almost as naked as they was born, damn it all Eve did wear a apron o'fig leaves in the Garden of Eden.'

Pre-1930 Standard Fordson tractor ploughing in the Vale of Evesham

My Land Girls stooking corn. Joyce is on the right

My first season with a combine-harvester

Some typical evacuees.
Right Helping to sack up
Savoy cabbages. *Below*
First meeting with the
village schoolmistress

Joyce making hay while the sun shines

The pig club flourished in wartime

Italian prisoners-of-war enjoy an English tea-break

Our wedding

Joyce in Land Army uniform

Market gardener with a setting
pin planting beans

Washing and tying radishes

Plum-picking in the Vale of Evesham, and loading the chip baskets
for market

The Home Guard of Ashton, Beckford, Hinton-on-the-Green and Sedgebarrow, outside Beckford village hall

Fordson Major tractor ploughing with a reversible plough at Ashton

Fordson County Crawler with a Ransome five-furrow plough

Tom Wheatcroft said that there was no need to panic. 'These girls knows more about nature than you think, and just because they be stripped off in the hot weather don't mean to say that they be more likely to slip up with a chap than the village wenches.'

Bert Amos had a note one morning that Daphne was not well enough to drive the tractor.

'Oi, it stands to sense,' Walt Gillet told him. 'Women be made different. Her ull let ya down, Bert, bwoy, as regular as the moon comes full over Broddy monument, I've never yeard tell of it, a 'ooman bouncing over the clods of clay cultivating the ground sat on a seat like a damn great meat dish.'

Meanwhile Carol Bennet's hairdresser from the Black Country came down to work for Mr. Bennet. She lived in at George Cowley's place at Merrylands. Audrey Miller was a girl of means who had to join something for the war effort. She had privileges denied the other girls, long weekends at home, arriving back on the 10.30 train on Monday mornings.

Henry Fanshaw met her at the station with the pony and governess cart. Audrey was like a piece of china. Neat in breeches and stockings, polished shoes, she helped Henry with the cows and calves, went with him to the Dog and Muffler most nights and drank beer like a foundry worker.

When Henry couldn't entertain her, Bill Brown met her at the Apple Tree. Then Sarah heard of it and left her husband to cook his own meals until once again peace was restored.

It was the recognised practice in Ashton for the regular women to finish work when the mangolds were pulled in November. The landgirls kept on throughout the winter, sprout-picking, threshing the corn, feeding the cattle and ploughing the stubbles.

Joyce and Doreen worked for me. One frosty morning they arrived to pick sprouts with Eric Packer and Tom Wheatcroft.

Tom looked at them as a father might have done and said, 'I don't know — it's never fitting this morning, you girls looks starved to death.'

'We have both had breakfast,' they said.

Tom was just speaking in his vernacular; he meant 'perished with cold'.

'They won't be yer five and twenty minutes,' Tom said. 'The older women be by the fire, that's where they ought to be.'

Doreen was from Wills of Bristol, Joyce had worked in an office at Dunlop Rubber Company.

I think the clear frosty air, although it was cold, did compensate a little for the smell of tobacco at Bristol and raw rubber at Dunlop's. Although Joyce worked in an office and not among the tyres, the smell could be unwelcome when the girls cycled up the drive on Monday mornings.

Really Annie Stephenson need not have been so irate when she spoke to Bert Amos about pay, because the girls were paid by the War Ag. and the farmer paid the War Ag. monthly.

One couldn't overestimate the value of these girls of the W.L.A. in producing food for the war effort.

It's true they were green, but a green stick will bend. No job came amiss to them, they were keen—too keen sometimes, like Sally when she put a bushel of wheat in the manger to feed the horse she was working with, when she came home at teatime. It was lucky Bill Brown was there in time before the corn was eaten, or else Mr. Bennet would have had one Suffolk Punch less, for wheat swells in the horse's stomach and kills.

Nancy, who worked at the next village, remarked to me that they would be busy in the spring because her boss had planted nearly all his farm with onions. I laughed and explained that it was wheat, but I must confess that both look very similar in the autumn when first they break through the earth.

The work in the fields before the war was done to a rhythm. The staid farm worker appeared to the outside world as being slow in his speech, his movements, his decisions.

The land girls changed all this. On my farm it was as if a holiday crowd had arrived anxious for everything to be done quickly.

I suppose that I was lucky, being young and able to cope with unskilled willing workers. Many an older man was impatient as

he stood on the rick at threshing time, and instead of the
sheaves being tossed by the pitchfork at his feet, butt end
first (that is to say, the end opposite the ears of corn) and
dropped one at a time, these girls were so anxious to get the
job done quickly they what we call mowed the old man with
a heap of sheaves, some facing in one way, some another, until
he turned his brown leathery face towards the middle of the
rick and said, 'Damned if I thought it ud come to this, working
yer with these city wenches.'

Gradually they got the hang of it all and found out that
thrashing was not a factory job, a conveyor belt.

When the War Ag. thresher brought its own labour force
of girls, one farmer refused to have them on his place.

'Tight as a duck's ass,' Jim Hicks called him.

When at last the tractor driver persuaded him that he must
work with them, 'Oi,' Skemer said, 'he reminds me of the
mon as kept the shop years ago. Bless ya, he'd cut a caraway
seed in half to get just the weight.'

Lunch-time on this farm brought no tea or coffee for the
girls, just a can of water to drink.

'Worse than when I was in Wales,' Jim told me. 'We did
have skim milk but no cider.'

When the team of girls had threshed my ricks and worked
hard until 3.30 I sent them home.

My neighbour found them work until five o'clock pulling
swedes, turnips or mangolds. He watched them through a gap
in the hedge. The one called Dorothy spotted him, walked
up to the hedge, pushed her blue eyes towards his beady brown
ones and shouted 'Snap'.

The mangold field rang with laughs from the girls and the
men.

This employer was so mean that instead of paying hire on
too many empty sacks hired from the Railway for threshing,
his man had to fill each sack to the brim, and he sewed the top
together with string instead of the usual tie of string at the
mouth. Then the swearing came when the lorry men were

expected to haul two-hundredweight-and-a-half of wheat instead of two-hundredweight-and-a-quarter, just to save a few shillings on sack hire.

I saw Land Girls doing all sorts of jobs, but the specials, as we called them, were the Rat Catchers or Rodent Operators.

They were a class apart dressed in immaculate breeches. Made up like film stars, they daintily put poison down rat holes on my farm with long-handled spoons. The girl in charge drove a green van, she never got out, but spent her time making up in the mirror, and polishing her nails.

A whiff of Soir de Paris or some such concoction met me when she left her driving seat at last for me to sign the book to say that they had been to the farm.

Some days later they came again. We dug away the muck bury and found that the spoonfuls of harmless-looking meal had proved lethal. Rats of all sizes had paid the penalty of taking the bait.

A necessary function these girls performed but they had an edge on them, so unlike the others. It seemed to me that they were not unlike the gas chamber crew over the water. When I mentioned Belsen to them in fun they pursed their red lips, put on more powder and left uncreased, clean as a pin with enough poison in the van to exterminate the rodent population of our country.

I remember I paid five pounds a year to the War Ag. for their services. Wheat was thirteen shillings a hundredweight, so it saved me money and saved wheat to bake the bread for the workers.

Land Girls did play a major part in our war effort. It seemed to me that with the older men as tutors and the boys leaving school, the land was worked better during the war than it had been in my lifetime.

It was good to see the rickyards full again, full of wheat, oats and barley ricks. Here, where the nettles had grown over the old staddle stones, the tidy sheaves were stacked.

How often would the folk in the munition factories have

been glad of the life on the farms, but it was not all the scent of new-mown hay, the sprouts were cold to handle on frosty mornings.

The Land Girls soon proved that any job a man could do they could do as well and sometimes better. But as young Len Wilkes and Eric Packer cycled up to the hostel on the hill where the girls lived, Sammy Bosworth winked at Jim Hicks, cleared his throat and said, 'Ah, there will no doubt be some bastard kids about here soon. Oi, the 'mericans be come to Ashchurch, and you knows what they gets up to.'

I just don't know whether these two men were disappointed there were no bastard kids, but the Americans did provide amusement if you like for the Land Girls at the Saturday night hops in the village hall.

Their gaudy uniforms, crepe-soled shoes and Camel cigarettes, their chocolate were all part of the wooing of the girls.

'Take a breather, honey', was a favourite invitation to the night air from the rattle of drums, the wail of the saxophone, the beat of the piano in the hall. Here the dust rose from the floorboards as the vocalists sang 'The Stars at night are shining bright, deep in the heart of Texas'; here Annie Stephenson, Flo Gillet and Sarah Brown sat on the chairs near the wall and knitted. It's true the wool was khaki for balaclava helmets for the troops, but what they said of Daphne, Christine, Sally and Wendy when they 'took a breather' with the G.I.s no-one ever knew.

Annie Stephenson soon made it her business to tell Sammy Bosworth of the goings on at the dances. Sammy was reckoned to be religious, but in so many cases when a man is too serious about his religion it means he's not too sure of it. Sammy talked of reading his title clear to mansions in the skies, but was anxious to hang on to the title deeds of his freehold on earth. He spoke of 'The worldly folk' and also of the next world.

Audrey Miller, ex-hairdresser, was a ravishing beauty among the girls. She soon had Henry Fanshaw around her little finger.

No dusty threshing of wheat and barley for her, but a place in Henry's newly-built office answering 'phone calls from the War Ag. and working out the wages. Flick Fanshaw was jealous, not without reason. That sleek fourteen horse-power car of Henry's took Audrey to a rather nice hotel on Friday nights. Here Audrey spent her wages, wages she never needed, for her business still flourished in the Black Country where ladies too old to help in the war effort did perms for officers' wives. No doubt Audrey was flattered by such attention, but how was Henry allowed petrol? That was easy, just a couple of bags of potatoes in the boot for the hotel and P.C. Wood could do nothing.

As usual Sammy and Jim thought the worst but there was no affair, as they say, just the fast car, the gin and tonic which elated the hairdresser in an alien world.

I thought it quite a coincidence that the girls from Wills' factory at Bristol should be living in a house among the orchards on the hill built by one of the original Wills family.

The hostel was a home with a view of the Cotswolds. Here one of the men who managed a farm in the next village had to start the engine every few days to charge the batteries to make electricity. Then as hot water was scarce at the house built for one family and not a lot of Land Girls, a War Ag. lorry took the girls to Pershore on Friday. Friday night was bath night.

I have a feeling that these new landworkers might not have settled down to country life had it not been for the influx of American soldiers. You see the Americans were at a loose end for company, and God knows how little entertainment or relaxation existed in our village for folk who had everything in the town.

And so on summer evenings the brass and khaki of the men from the other side of the Atlantic graced our country lanes and Daphne, Christine, Sally and Wendy walked through the bridle path gate at the bottom of the orchards and spent the evenings in Uncle Sam's arms away from the hoeing and picking of beans and peas, the climbing of ladders among the plum plantations of the Vale.

Eric Packer, who now drove my new Fordson and turned the turf with a Canadian cockshutt plough, showed a blonde from Wills' factory the beauties of the hill after he had changed from his navy boiler suit into the conventional sports coat and flannels.

One Sunday evening as I strolled down our village from Chapel I met Olive. I had spoken to her before on the Evesham bus. There was something different about her speech as she walked pushing her bike with me through three villages before I realised that I would have to walk all the way back home. It was just that a Private School had got rid of the Worcestershire burr, and as Uncle George would have said, she talked flash.

At the Roman Catholic Church corner she said as we parted, 'You can't kiss me tonight, but if we meet on Saturday you can.'

At tea-time on Saturday Mother sensed that, after a bath from the harvesting, the amount of Brylcream on my hair was above the usual and the shine of my shoes had an extra glow.

'Who are you seeing tonight then, Fred?' she asked, as I pushed my Hercules bike down the drive.

'Oh just someone I know a few villages away, a Land Girl.'

Mother went back into our house and it was hard to say whether she was annoyed, amused or glad. I knew that she had hoped I'd marry Janet, the chubby Cheltenham girl, who used to sing solos at the Chapel and won prizes for her singing, but that was not to be.

'How about the flicks, say, at the Sabina at Tewkesbury, and can I call you Freddy?' Olive asked.

A new word to a village chap was 'flicks'. So we cycled to the town, had tea at a place known as the Ancient Grudge and to the flicks we went. Don't ask me what we saw, but I remember the red suede jacket and emerald green corduroy skirt which gave Olive an edge over the usual cinema goers of the town. Then the ride back with blacked out bicycle lamps under the stars. The halt at the roadside gate where Sunday's promise was kept and supper at her mother's hillside cottage and the promise of a meeting on Wednesday night.

Olive picked fruit from the trees planted by the famous Raymond Bush. Cox's Orange Pippins were weighing down the half-standard trees.

On Wednesday we walked the path through the apple orchards. Then we both sat on the gate and munched two crisp, juicy apples Olive had left there, a treat in war-time.

She told me of her ex-boy friend shot down in the R.A.F. over Hamburg; she was fond of him. In a clumsy way I told her and showed her how fond I was of her.

It's not usual for courting couples to judge their partner as they did years ago when the girl had to prove herself fit for a farmer's wife by lifting the heavy lid of the church chest, but I do recall vividly the muscles of my partner's arms. How strong they looked below the short sleeves of her Viyella shirt. 'The ground needs squeezing hard like a young woman,' Jim Hicks always said. I suppose a young chap fancies his strength, but the days of fruit picking, the weeks of threshing corn, had given Olive a come-hither grip which was good to feel after the half-hearted embraces which we all go through.

It's true a girl who is warm-hearted and vivacious has something difficult to explain in words. The Bible says that there is nothing quite so wonderful as the way of a man with a maid. I would reverse that because the opposite sex have a disarming force which lifts a fellow like me high above the hill.

We sat at midnight on the wooden bench by the Tower, we listened to our 'planes going and coming from the nearby 'dromes. One night we had supper at Sheldon Farm with some Jewish refugees who worked on the estate. They were homely folk but had a forlorn look as they told us of their friends in Germany.

'I'll leave you a minute, Freddy, just half a sec,' and Olive jumped over a Cotswold stone wall into a coppice. I waited in the ride between the trees. A vixen squealed just like a baby.

To hear a vixen on the still night when hardly a leaf moved on the trees, the only sound being Olive's footsteps as the twigs cracked underfoot, is alarming.

Olive called out 'Freddy!' I ran towards her and she did to me what Jim Hicks said the ground needed, she squeezed and held on all the way down the hill for home. My mischievous thoughts thanked that vixen for bringing us so close together that night.

Chapel on Sunday, and as Olive listened with me to a man from a neighbouring village she tittered.

'How dare she!' Mother said, but my Land Army girl knew that Mr. X was no better than he should be, and for him to put himself on a pedestal and talk down at us was too much.

Dad liked Olive; he liked anyone who worked hard in fact. Mother was not impressed by her appetite for the flicks and dances. She told me once that no-one was ever up to any good after midnight, but we had fun together in the dark years when Evesham Station was blacked out and we had an empty carriage on the last train from the flicks at the Clifton. But with so much to do on the farm and so few hands to help, our meetings became less frequent, and the old saying is true that if you have a friendship it must be fostered regularly, the parties must meet or else they drift apart. We drifted. I was quite comfortable at home and Olive married a G.I. and went to the States. He was one of the nicest Americans at Ashchurch, I'm glad because she did deserve a good partner.

So ended a little chapter in life which I recall with a smile, sitting back and becoming more and more conscious of the unassuming make-up of youth. Youth when the physical strength is at its peak, yet the power to express, the ability to understand the finer points in nature are immature.

Daphne ploughed a particularly heavy piece of land for me with Thomas Bennet's crawler tractor. The autumn leaves were scattering from the headland elms but the sun had still most of its summer power. I sat and shared ten o'clock lunch with her. We talked of the new film at the Regal, and on the following Saturday afternoon we stood together in an hour long queue to see 'Gone with the Wind', a long film where we sat spell bound watching Scarlet O'Hara in Glorious Technicolour, Daphne's hair was bleached by the summer sun, she looked different when not in uniform, she was the sort of girl who looked her best when not dressed up. The lipstick and powder robbed her of the freshness of the outdoor girl she had become. We sat towards the front; we had to, the queue pushed us there, and the screen looked high above. Daphne squeezed my hand when the amputations were performed by the doctor without anaesthetic but that was the only reason she did squeeze — we would never have loved each other, somehow the distance between our real selves was much too great. A nice girl, however, a nice evening.

The Americans came to every camp and airfield around us. The produce of the Vale flowed in lorries to the canteens. They hated brussels sprouts but must have eaten an awful lot.

Joyce and Doreen, Eric and Tom picked my sprouts. They picked on some winter mornings when the frost made the sprout leaves droop like half closed umbrellas.

I loaded the nets on my little lorry and took them to market.

The girls were paid by the War Ag. so it was only right to pay them the little extra piecework of so much per net which Eric and Tom were paid.

Picking together into one net holder, Joyce and Doreen usually picked and carried to the headland fifty nets per day.

What did Annie, Flo and Sarah think, I wonder? But as the spring came and the last corn rick was thrashed, the cattle turned out into the field and the lambs growing every day under the apple blossom, Doreen, who had married a Private in the Somerset Light Infantry, told me she was leaving.

'Why?' I said.

'To take up part-time work.'

Tom Wheatcroft grinned and said to Doreen, 'I reckon the job you will have ull be full time.'

Blushing, she admitted that a happy event was expected. She left in early May.

When the sheep were ready to shear by late May, I bought a Lister sheep-shearing machine from Gloucester and tried my hand at taking the fleeces from 120 ewes. Joyce provided the power by turning the handle of the machine, a job she did from morning until night on her twenty-first birthday.

My collie dog was run over by a convoy of lorries on the main road. Skipper was worth a lot to me farming the sheep, driving them from field to field when the bluebottle fly became busy laying its yellow eggs on the soiled backsides of the lambs. In twenty-four hours the maggots hatched out, sending the lambs in circles around the field, irritated, sometimes sulky, but once seen never forgotten. Joyce helped me hurdle the sheep, while I clipped the soiled wool from around lambs' tails and applied Jeyes Fluid to kill the maggots.

On steaming hot days in June after overnight rain this was a daily job until the dipping kept off 'the blue assed fly' as Tom called it.

Dorothy took Doreen's place. A jolly girl from Walsall who laughed every morning away, mornings after she had spent the evening before with the Americans. Dorothy was a Frank Sinatra fan, she sang his songs in the fields, her Black Country accent pronounced. Another good worker, although a slip of a girl of eighteen.

That summer was so hot that the hayfields were cut one day with the mower by Eric and me and the hay was fit to carry the next day. The girls in shorts and shirts were as brown as the parched earth itself.

'Unt natural,' Jim Hicks said. 'They plasters their legs with Camp coffee.'

Of course Jim was wrong. This was understandable, for Annie, Flo and Sarah wore long skirts, black stockings and lace up boots. It's like Tom Wheatcroft always said, 'That which ull keep the cold out ull keep the heat out.'

When the ricks of wheat were built by Tom I stayed and

shared tea with Joyce in the harvest field. The War Ag. spam sandwiches and red so-called tomato sauce and processed cheese was a monotonous diet.

From the pig killing we had basins of lard at home, lard flavoured with rosemary. I took extra for a snack under the wheat rick. Joyce fancied home rendered lard on the bread and I was glad of her company.

As the winter nights drew in I cycled to the hostel and met her. We walked and sat and talked for hours under the thatched wheat ricks. There seemed common interests between us. Joyce was a Methodist and she liked the country life. I'd been brought up a Baptist then a fundamentalist (whatever that means). This meant that when I was invited to her home at Sutton Coldfield, the service, the hymns, the beliefs were what I was used to, while Joyce found the same of our Chapel in the village. So, as the saying is, we were going steady.

After walking the endless acres of Sutton Park among the pools, holly and the gorse, the next weekend would be spent at our house. I suppose that Bredon Hill was similar when we reached the plateau on the top. Windswept, bare and bleak above the hostel, the old quarries had left the land in bowls of turf pared short by the rabbits. In spring the hill was alive with them; in the evenings here the foxes came close to us as we nestled in the hollows and watched the sun set over Herefordshire.

Saturday nights we travelled back on Mr. Buchanan's bus, which was loaded. To say 'loaded' is an understatement, it was bursting at the seams.

A bus built for twenty passengers brought home the villagers, the groceries, the couples from the cinema at Evesham including Joyce and me. There was no time for any dissent in the village then, as Barbara was squeezed against Joan and Cynthia sat on Harry's lap. With the bus down on the springs George Buchanan steered his cargo over the river bridge and without fail we landed safe at the village cross.

It's true the war was a great leveller. Gentlemen who had

owned cars had no petrol, they came on the local bus to and from the town, sat beside the cowman and tractor drivers and the Land Girls.

Working together by day and on our nightly outings Joyce and I got to know each other pretty well. It's odd looking back how things worked out. Mrs. Mingaye, a lady of more than eighty, died in one of Dad's cottages. The cottage was modernised to the extent of indoor sanitation instead of the little house covered with ivy up the garden. It had been empty about a month when I popped the question to Joyce.

I think she was surprised and I'm sure that my words were not at all eloquent when that spring evening at nearby Grafton I asked her to marry me.

Neither of us was the sort to make snap decisions, but on 19th May we bought an engagement ring in Cheltenham, had tea at the Cadena and I dared Joyce to wear it. A party from our village sat at the next table, but we were officially engaged at Sutton Coldfield the next day on her birthday.

And so the usual wartime struggle to get furniture at sales, and buy curtains. I remember buying an old settee for £27 at a sale in Malvern and bringing it home on the roof rack of the car, and this with a utility dining suite filled up the dining room. The little lounge had to wait.

A wartime wedding was a ploy which had to be arranged long before the event. The rations were hoarded, the cake arrived from somewhere, even the flowers were in profusion. My in-laws arranged the whole thing to perfection.

I remember cutting myself shaving that morning and seeing Joyce come down the aisle on her Dad's arm looking beautiful in the wedding dress which we had such difficulty in buying.

My black coat and waistcoat, pinstripe trousers, which cost £5 before the war for Tom's wedding, still fitted me.

It was good to get away in the taxi to the station and board the train for Llandudno.

I wonder, did everyone feel like this? Quite a few Land Girls did marry farmers. It's not for me to say why, except that farmers do like a partner who is interested in crops and stock, and many city girls when they once taste the country air never want to return to the bright lights where they came from. This yen, this hankering after country life, exists in lots of large towns. Is this because two or three generations ago these folk were living in country villages?

When the wedding guests of today are invited to come round and look at the wealth of presents, I often think of those days when a tablecloth from Sammy Bosworth was for Sundays only and a prized possession of our cottage home.

9

How the News Got Through

WHEN I WAS A BOY VILLAGE FOLK OFTEN SAID TO ME: 'It's bound to be true because it's in the papers.'

We all knew how different newspapers look at news from their own angle.

In the war the papers were bound by law to use restraint in reporting international and national events. For the first time ever a world war was coming over as news on the radio. War in the past had glamour. Battles were fought on foreign fields, in English villages people lived isolated from the outside world.

We read in history books of how men fought men in shining

armour. Even in the 1914 War the aeroplane had not the range or power that it had now achieved.

Despite the mass slaughter of the prime of mankind on the Somme in the First World War, soldiers told us of the Christmas Day truce, of the Angel of Mons. So up until now war was looked upon in something the same way as a virtuous spinster thinks of wickedness. All right to talk about as long as it doesn't come too near.

Harvey, an old friend now dead, once told me of the Christmas Day in France when the British and Germans celebrated together. This young German chap, he said, was in a trench about fifty yards from him.

'Happy Christmas, Tommy,' he said, offering me a fag.

'Same to thee, Jerry,' I said, and we shared some bully beef, sang a few carols and I thought how damn silly we was to fight.

It was like it all along the line, then about tea-time I turned to this yer Jerry and said: 'You know it breaks my heart to think that I got to shoot thee tomorrow.'

'*Neine, Neine*, me and you be friends, Tommy,' he said. 'No shoot me.'

'My orders be "to shoot", and thee bist in that trench oppisite so look out.'

Next morning when the fighting recommenced, Harvey, who was really a wag, saw the German's steel helmet above the trench.

He called out, 'Keep yer yud down or else I shall shoot ya' and to make his point clear he fired his magazine of bullets into a sandbag, as he said 'frightening the poor little devil very near to death'.

With radio now things were so different, different from when our newspaper boy walked up and down the village in the 1914–18 War selling the evening paper, *The Echo*, and shouting: 'Biggest ship of the Germans sunk, *The Blucher*.'

The ritual of listening in lasted for some folk from seven o'clock in the morning until ten o'clock at night.

No-one dared speak when the wireless news was on. One had to read between the lines when the anonymous announcer said that some of our bombers failed to return from their raid.

Winston Churchill kept us all optimistic on his Sunday-night broadcasts. Our 'planes, he promised, would bring the Nazis to their knees. Yet our 'planes were so few and the opposition so enormous. We learnt after how a few brave men saved these islands with Spitfires and Hurricanes.

There were some funny interpretations of news items. Charlie Stephenson met Henry Fanshaw one morning as Bert Amos was taking the horses to the corn field.

'My goy, gaffer,' he said, 'they be going at it out in Iterly. Hammer and tongs they be at it, our chaps be advancing on all sexes, the women be fled to Rome.'

'Rome unt in Italy,' Walt Gillet said in a knowing way.

'I never said it was, did I, ya silly crater,' Charlie replied.

Bennet's bailiff laughed as Sarah Brown reported that according to the seven o'clock news there had been very little activity during the night.

'You speak for yourself, missus,' Charlie said. 'Oi, you speak for yourself.'

Then Bill Brown gave Lord Haw Haw's latest scare.

'Ashchurch camp they be gwain to bomb and he said that they have damn near wiped out our Air Force.'

'What, agun?' Charlie said as he stood by the stable door waiting for the horses to finish drinking at the iron trough.

'He reckoned that they was wiped out last wick, the liar.'

Then we heard J. B. Priestley regularly trying to cheer us up on the radio. We looked forward to the society we should have after the war, a soothing Yorkshire voice which served a good purpose just as Ralph Wightman did from Dorset.

The radio was a bright spot in the evening, home from the fields, when Tommy Handley and Jack Warner still had a lot to make us laugh about. Jack Warner's letters from Brother Syd were memorable.

The war was almost worldwide, yet the need for secrecy

gave us the feeling that the very hedges which marked our parish boundary were vital. This parish was what our young men were fighting for.

The Home Guard were guarding, and why should outsiders be told how many tons of potatoes we had 'buried up', or what wheat ricks remained to be thrashed?

'Be like Dad, keep Mum' read the posters in the railway carriages.

It was in a way a similar position to the time of Napoleon when we took no census of population because he would then have known exactly how many there were of us he was up against.

And so the finger posts were taken down, making it difficult to find the way anywhere by car.

Our villages were often loth to tell a stranger the way to another village. 'Like enough they be enermy spies,' Skemer told me. 'It yunt worth the risk. One chap, and I didn't like the look on him, in a posh car wanted to know the road to Tewkesbury. I sent him to Evesham road, you never know, he might a bin one of Lord Haw Haw's men going to spy Aschurch camp. I never did trust strangers,' Skemer said, 'not since some smart Alec done me down at Evesham Mop Fair wrapping up and putting gold watches in envelopes and charging a bob a piece. I bought a envelope with only a tie pin inside. No, Frederick, strangers beunt to be trusted.'

10

Nothing But Weeds

THE PLOUGH LAND YIELDED FAIRLY WELL FOR THE
first two years of the war. The summers were hot and the
wheat ripened hard in the stook.

Jim Hicks and Will Richardson still planted the corn with
two horses and the five-furrow drill.

'I beunt gone on Master Bennet's new combine drill,' Jim
said. 'It don't put the seed in dip enough for me. Fanshaw and
them Land Army wenches be in and out of the field and now
Audrey drives one a them rubber-tyred tractors.'

'What about it?' I asked him.

Jim raised his eyebrows and sighed a deep sigh as he muttered: 'Too fast. It wouldn't of done for the old Squire,' he added, 'driving across the field with a Cambridge roll, hell for leather. It stands to sense the ground unt worked that a road, thee wait and see when the thunder storms come in July.'

I waited. One field of Mr. Bennet's was so foul with weeds as the moist muggy weather persisted. The wheat went flat under the heavy rain. Charlock, pig weed, may weed and cleavers showed green among the rows of laid corn.

Henry Fanshaw came along with a new reaper and binder power-driven off the power taken from one of his tractors.

Audrey drove around the field, her tractor pulling the binder. Harry sat on the binder seat operating the levers.

It was after tea when they started and no road had been cut with the hooks. 'Opening up for the machine' we called it.

'No time for that,' Fanshaw said, and he showed Jim Hicks, who leant on the gate with Will, the farmer's paper where a farmer stated that if the tractor runs over the standing corn, the corn can be cut near the hedge by cutting a back swath like mowing the hay.

As the rubber-tyred wheels flattened still more of the crop, Jim was almost speechless, just muttering under his breath, 'When folks like them two craters be born I suppose they got to be kept.'

Harry's binder, with the fingers and knife pointed down towards the ground and sometimes digging into the soil, cut the said corn and weeds. The sheaves were untidy, full of what Jim called rait and pelf.

After some weeks in the stooks the sheaves dried out. The stooking was done by Daphne, Christine and Sally. Eight sheaves put together in one stook. The soft hands and polished finger nails of the factory and office were now so different, but despite the hardened skin the thistles pricked their hands like thousands of needles.

'Young Henry and that fancy wench on the tractor ought to handle the sheaves,' Jim told Sammy Bosworth. 'Now if they'ud plant it with the five-furrow drill and not been in such a damned hurry, the crop would have stood up to the weather.'

On his weekend visit from Birmingham Thomas Bennet viewed the fields as the corn stood up in aisles some yards apart waiting for the fine weather, and the men to come and pitch the sheaves into his tractor trailers.

Carol, his young wife, walked with him on a fine Sunday evening in September.

'Darling,' she said, 'you know this field here called The Langet? It's awfully rough, the corn, I mean, and have you seen our poor girls' hands, how the thistles have inflamed them?'

'Quite,' Thomas said, 'I'll have a word with Fanshaw.'

At Rosemary Cottage Flick Fanshaw asked Henry's master into the front room.

'My husband won't be a minute. I believe he's shaving, some idea of meeting that Audrey Miller off the evening train later in his car.'

'Audrey,' Carol said, 'I do hope she's not suffered with the thistles in her hands.'

'Not likely, Mrs. Bennet, your hairdresser rides a tractor. Henry won't let her handle thistles.'

That moment the bailiff of Partridge Farm came into the room, clean-shaven, smelling of Brylcream.

'By gad, Fanshaw, are you off to a wedding or something?'

Carol interrupted her husband. 'After all, darling, it is Sunday night.'

Thomas Bennet was not very pleased.

'Look here, Fanshaw,' he said, 'I want an explanation about the crop in the Langet, it's damn near all weeds.'

'The other fields, are they up to your expectations, sir?'

Henry meekly said, 'Yes, if it's fine get the men and tractors and start carting the wheat to the rickyard tomorrow.'

'I was going to do that, weren't we, Flick?' Henry replied and Flick nodded.

'The rubbish you have grown in the Langet is not to come into my rickyard, understand?'

Thomas was now quite red under his collar.

'You build a rick in the field and thrash it as soon as possible, and don't you realise, Fanshaw, that my friends will be down for the partridge shoot in a couple of weeks and I'm not going to be made a laughing stock by the other farmers or the War Ag.'

'I see,' Henry said, looking at Flick. 'I'm ashamed of that field.'

'Ashamed,' Mr. Bennet replied. 'The War Ag. could make ours a B registered farm for that and me in my position.'

The wheat was stacked with its weeds in a corner of the Langet field after the best corn had been ricked in the rickyard.

'Be ya gwain to thrash that yup of rubbish?' Charlie Stephenson asked Henry one damp morning when the steam was rising from the pile in the Langet.

Henry shook his head and replied,

'I don't know what to do.'

'I'll tell ya what,' Charles suggested. 'Shall I'll sham thatch him, now I finished the t'others?'

'Sham thatch,' the Agricultural College man replied. 'What on earth is that?'

'Leave it to me. All I want is a load of straw and some rick pegs and I'll show you.'

George pegged the straw on the roof of the rick, just enough to keep off the heavy rain, with a few strands of binder twine; the job was soon finished.

By late October the steam no longer came from the rick. The heat of the green stuff, the weeds, had died down, the threshing drum arrived. Charles, Walt, Bill, the girls and Henry made up the gang.

As the sheaves were pitched into the drum and Daphne cut the strings, the dust was unbelievable.

'Smoke screens they puts up in the army, I thought,' Walt shouted above the noise of the threshing drums, as he stood waiting for a sack of two hundredweight. A quarter was full, but also a sack of weeds came from the spout where the rubbish came from.

Walt delved his hand down among the weed seeds and looked puzzled at the variety.

'Thurs enough thristles, docks, pig weed and charlock, cleavers, Lord knows what's in this yer rick, to plant Bredon Hill. What be I to do with it, Bailiff?'

Walt shouted to Henry who stood among the dusty sheaves.

'Put the sacks of wheat on a trailer, stack the weed seeds and then we can put a rick sheet over it. We don't want Mr. Bennet to know how much rubbish we have grown in the Langet.'

That night when the hum of the threshing machine was still in the workers' ears the poor cast or yield of grain was safe in the barn at Partridge Farm, the weeds lay in sacks under a tarpaulin sheet in the Langet field. No doubt Jim Hicks and nosey Sammy Bosworth went along after dark and with dimmed torches counted the cost of Henry's mistake and talked of it in the village.

Thomas Bennet and Carol took an autumn holiday in Scotland, they had friends there. Henry knew that they would be away for a fortnight which pleased him in several ways. He didn't want the Birmingham business man to know how much weed had been threshed in the Langet.

One weekend he read in a farming paper an advert. for bird seed from a firm in East London.

'I'm going to London,' he told Flick, 'to sell the weeds we threshed. Weed seeds for bird feed are worth more than best milling wheat.'

Flick looked disinterested as she said,

'I suppose you are taking that hairdresser. You take her, I don't care.'

'Well,' Henry said, 'I need someone to unload the sacks at the other end.'

'I suppose you know that your petrol ration does not include trips to London with Land Girls.'

Henry just stood and stared.

On Monday morning as Bert Amos fed his horses in the

stable the bailiff told him that he was in charge of Partridge Farm for a few days.

'What, me?' Bert said, 'what about if the gaffer comes down from Brum?'

'He won't,' Henry explained that he was gone to Scotland on holiday. 'But you know just what to do, you and one of the girls can drill the winter wheat on the summer fallow. Charles and Walt must go on with the apple picking and start pulling the mangolds, Bill Brown and Ralph Simms, now I'd like them to start hedge laying in the big ground. You, Bert, can show Daphne how to plough the stubble.'

'It depends on the weather, there's plenty to do. How long are you going away for, Henry?' Bert stuttered.

Henry said that it depended on how he got on selling the bird seed in London.

The morning Charles and Walt loaded Henry's big Austin 16 with sacks of weed seeds they loaded the big cattle trailer with sacks until all the heap in the Langet was cleared.

'Just a minute before we start, Audrey. I want a couple of bags of potatoes in the boot.'

'Taters, Walt?' Charles said with a laugh. 'He ull want more than taters to cope with that wench.'

Up Broadway Hill with the illicit load the Austin headed for Oxford and the smoke.

'Some address in Camberwell we want, Audrey, and don't forget if a policeman stops us it's clover seed in the sacks.'

Audrey smiled, 'Henry dear, you think of everything.'

In a backyard at Camberwell, where a whole street once stood, piles of bricks and rubble showed the effect of the German bombs.

'Right, mate, I got your message. You are Mr. Fanshaw, pleased to see ya, I'm Syd, this is my pal Harry, we deal in anything that's short like, and it's for cash.'

Harry climbed onto the trailer, gave a wink to Syd as he opened a sack and told Henry that they would do business.

'Thirty sacks,' Henry said, 'and nice and dry.'

'Free hundred quid, I reckon,' Syd said.

'Make it three-fifty, we have come a long way.'

Henry thought he would try it on anyway.

'Free-fifty it is,' Syd answered, grasping Henry's hand.

No, Audrey didn't soil her hands. Two doubtful-looking characters came from a smelly back kitchen and unloaded the sacks into an outhouse.

Syd counted out the fivers and agreed to let Henry leave his car in the yard. Henry didn't want to be driving around London with an empty trailer.

'It's time for a meal in town,' Henry suggested to Audrey, 'and we can stay a few days up here.'

'Where?' Audrey said.

'Not at the Salvation Army when I've £350 in my wallet. We will find a place, Mrs. Fanshaw.'

'Mrs. Fanshaw? But really we shan't book in as man and wife, Henry.'

Of course Bert Amos, Bill Brown and Flick thought that all at once Henry had gone off the rails. London's a place of secrets so no-one knew what happened the week they were away. All that's known is that Henry put two bags of potatoes from the car boot into the trailer to bring back to Ashton.

It looked better with petrol rationed to see a breeched and gaitered farm bailiff with two hundredweight of potatoes in his trailer.

Meanwhile what was happening in our village at Ashton? Flick was attractive, young, vivacious. Some American service men had often been to Rosemary Cottage and spent an evening there. A captain from the army camp at Ashchurch was a frequent visitor.

While Henry was in London he came most evenings.

Jim Hicks, who lived opposite, was very interested when the big car arrived. He described to me the goings on, as he called them, which he had watched from his bedroom window.

'First of all a big joint of best beef is carried in, then the bottles of intoxicating liquor.' No doubt Jim was jealous when he said at the Apple Tree pub that 'it didn't become a young 'ooman like Flick to trade along with the Yanks'.

The atmosphere at Partridge Farm was tense when the Austin 16 came back from London.

Flick was not exactly pleased to see Henry back, she had had a good time with her American, Lew. Lew was a single man, a farmer from California. Flick was the first woman he had really loved, he intended her to be the only woman.

Flick's opinion of Henry had changed. His father, a London stockbroker, had pressed him into farming. Farming for him was a little better than the army, no more.

Thomas Bennet arrived back from Scotland to find the wheat safe in his barns, but was not surprised at the low yield from the Langet.

'Where is all that rubbish which came from the threshing drum in the Langet, Henry?' the master of Partridge Farm asked him. 'I hope you have burnt it. We don't want all that weed seed spread over our land and don't forget the Langet has to be cleaned next year to lie fallow, then ploughed and cultivated until it looks as if it belongs to me.'

Henry took £250 out of his wallet. 'Here you are, sir. I sold the seed for the canaries up in London.'

'Damn it, Fanshaw, you have a better head on your shoulders than I imagined. Did you go alone?'

'Not quite,' Henry confessed, 'I took Audrey.'

Thomas Bennet pursed his lips, then looked his bailiff straight in the face and laughed, clutching the £250.

'Well, I suppose all's fair in love and war,' he said. 'What about Flick?'

'Oh, she's been well looked after by Captain Lew from Aschurch, all very complicated.'

'Now look here, Fanshaw,' Thomas replied, 'I'm not interfering with your private life as long as the work's done, understand. This farm has got to remain as a farm, and I'm relying on you to look after it.'

For months after Henry still took Audrey to the Dog and

Muffler in the evenings and Lew spent his leave time at Rosemary Cottage.

Then Lew was posted to the Far East. Flick was broken-hearted, but really Henry did think the world of her despite his attraction to Audrey.

II

The Italian Prisoners

'HOW MANY MORE INTERLOPERS BE GWAIN TO COME to this yer parish?' Jim Hicks said to Sammy Bosworth one morning when an army lorry unloaded the brown battle-dressed, dark-skinned remnants of Mussolini's army. It's true the Italian Army was still fighting, but a good number of prisoners of war came over here to help with the work on the land.

'Light patches on the ass of the trousers, I see they got,' Jim pointed out to Skemer as they met in the road.

'Oi, and singing they be down in our barn,' Skemer reported on my first two P.O.W.s, Peter and Joe.

Sammy Bosworth decided to have two also.

Jim Hicks was really upset.

'What,' he said, 'Himploy them sods as bin killing our bwoys out in Hitterly. I beunt a gwain to work along them Ities.'

Every morning at eight o'clock the army lorries stopped up our village street.

'Bon giorno, boss,' Joe shouted as he jumped off the tailboard of the army vehicle and carried his overcoat and packed lunch into my yard.

The chatter on the lorry was as excited as that of a load of children off on a Sunday School outing.

Jim Hicks soon came to terms with Sammy's men, Septembre and Hectorine.

Bert Amos sometimes had trouble with his team. Thomas Bennet employed about ten, which gave the Italians the benefit of one man allowed to cook at midday. They did pretty well, rabbits were plentiful and the prisoners were allowed an extra cheese ration like other farm workers, even the farmers were not allowed that.

So the music of Naples, Venice, Sicily and Rome rang through our streets from the morning lorry and in the fields.

'Like a lot of flaming jackdaws a-chattering round the gargoyles of the church,' Skemer told me, 'I unt having much cotter along with um,' he said when he sat apart under the hedge with his bread and cheese.

'Skemer,' Joe called. 'You like cigarettee very good from camp.'

'Oi,' Skemer said, stirring from his seat on a sack. 'But don't thee tell the missus, I beunt allowed to smoke at home.'

'Me no understand much Englise.' 'Pogi pogi just a little,' said Joe as Skemer puffed at the cigarette.

Joe turned to me and said,

'Boss, why prisoners no have some Players? Mr. Churchill smoke a big cigar.'

I laughed, knowing that if Joe and Peter stayed the work

would be done. But the camp authorities sometimes changed the men to different farms. Joe was very strong, a shorter version of Primo Carnero, the heavyweight boxer.

So it seemed to me that once more the Romans came to Britain, but this time things were different from when Nero told our ancestors what to do.

'They be some poor mothers' sons,' Annie Stephenson said to Flo Gillet as they passed my Cross Barn Orchard where Joe and Peter were picking apples, swaying on their ladders. Their singing in the breeze of an English autumn carried far from the trees, they sang when they were happy, sang when they were sad.

They were fearless fruit pickers and when Joe stood on the top rung but one on a forty-rung ladder I told him, 'Don't break your neck just for two apples on the highest bough, Joe.'

Joe, who seemed to understand some English, replied, 'Boss, no fear, if the ladder fall into the tree me fall too.'

He sang a sad song that day about a train standing in a station.

It is embarrassing to a degree to give praise to men who had been and still were our enemies, but I must speak as I find. The Italians were said to be lazy, mine were good workers at almost any farm job.

Henry Fanshaw tried with Bert Amos to drive his and treat them as cheap slave labour at a shilling an hour. They didn't work too well for him.

Sammy Bosworth got plenty of work from his two men.

'A drop of cider does the trick,' he told me.

As the apples were finished, two or three Pitmaston Duchess pear trees remained to be picked. I borrowed a fifty-rung ladder from Mr. Bennet. The wind blew a gale. Peter and Joe raised the ladder against the first tree.

'You pick the pears, Peter, you are lighter than Joe up the ladder, and Joe, you stand on the bottom rung to steady the ladder.'

Joe's dark brown eyes looked at me. He turned to Peter and said something which sounded like 'A lan a ma ramer on a dare na stare na.'

'No cabbise,' I replied, meaning I don't understand.

'Boss,' Joe said, 'Peter pick o pears, I no stand on ladder. What you think people of Ashton will say? They will say "Criste, that lazy bastard him no work." Boss, please can I work some other place?'

I took him to another pear tree, a Comice which he picked with a shorter ladder.

One lunch time Eric, Tom, Skemer and I, talked with our prisoners.

I said, 'Plenty talk, Joe, on the lorry this morning.'

Joe replied, 'Boss, you know something, we speak of different farmers, some good to work for, some bad. If a different prisoner go to work for a man who shouts and swears we tell him, him bad boss, you no do much work; if that man good boss, we say plenty work.'

Peter turned to Skemer who just grunted at the broken English and said, 'Skemer, if you take that horse there to water you cannot make him drink.'

Bill Brown was out in charge of Bennet's Italians. He coaxed them, showed them how to cut hedges, feed cattle, and cut and shape timber for Ralph Sims who made farm gates when he wasn't catching rabbits.

Bill was Thomas Bennet's salvation in lots of ways. Henry was eager to work, but so green. What he knew all came from book learning. Bill Brown left school at thirteen, could handle horses, mend implements, build ricks—an all-rounder.

Back on my farm I had eleven acres of sprouts fit to pick in October. Eric and Tom were busy planting the winter wheat with the tractor and converted corn drill. Converted from a shafted horse-drawn effort by putting a tractor draw-bar on instead.

Skemer pottered around the cattle, helped me with the sheep. This left the two Land Girls, Joyce and Doreen, to pick the sprouts. I applied to the War Ag. for more prisoners for a month or so.

They sent eight in addition to Joe and Peter, Fallovalita, Carnevarni, one they called Stalin who cooked the potata friet — chips in English.

So I went to the Army and Navy Stores and bought tarpaulin trousers and the War Ag. provided Wellingtons. Peter was our best picker, he had farmed land near Naples.

'One minoote, boss,' Joe said as I entered the field and weighed the nets of sprouts on the spring balance suspended from a rough wooden tripod known locally as the sticks.

'Trouble, Joe?' I said.

'No fear, boss, these cigarettes from camp similar straw?' Joe waved his hand to emphasise his point, then said, 'Boss, me like Players.'

I said, 'Yes, very good.'

I waited for Joe to tell me what I had already guessed.

'Boss,' he said, 'if you buy some Players for every ten nets we pick we plenty work, you plenty sprouts for market.'

'I pay the War Ag.,' I said, but that day in Evesham after the market I brought some packets of twenty Players cigarettes.

The words of Joe remained in my ears, 'Plenty Players plenty work.'

Joe and eight other men kept their promise.

Stalin was cook and was lazy, a dark man from Sicily who sulked, but as nine-tenths of the men were workers, we put up with Stalin.

When Italy capitulated the P.O.W.s arrived looking very sad.

'Finish war with Germany, Fallovalita go back to Italy, boss,' Fallovalita said sadly.

Joe winked at me saying, 'Boss, Fallovalita was a volunteer, me a conscript. Fallovalita no go back to Italy until war is finished with Japan.'

Peter and Joe then explained in Italian to him and Fallovalita must have sworn all day at his work, especially when Joe told him that the Americans in Italy would be having fun with his wife.

Joe was not married.

Up at Partridge Farm Henry Fanshaw tried all ways to make his prisoners work on the day of the capitulation of their army. Flick even tried to persuade her favourite charmer, Sebastian, but they all sat and moped.

Flick's American was gone for good, Henry still paid a great deal of attention to Audrey, so Sebastian, that dark, wavy-haired film-star-looking young man, who when he grinned showed a set of teeth (snow-white pearls) under a Ronald Colman moustache, soon became a favourite with Flick.

Every night when the lorry loaded the men and took them back to their camp on the golf course, Flick was sad to see Sebastian leave Partridge Farm. She persuaded Henry to let him stay in the Groom Bothy near the stable with another prisoner called Pasquale.

The War Ag. checked that the accommodation was suitable and soon the two moved in. They slept on camp beds, cooked on an oil stove and bathed once a week at Rosemary Cottage.

'Boss,' Joe said one day to me as he struggled up the Pike Ground carrying four nets of sprouts on his broad shoulders. 'Me and Peter would like to stay on the farm, me no like camp and the barbed wire.'

I wrote to the Commandant and said I had a building where I could billet two prisoners, Joe and Peter. An officer came and said that it would be suitable if there was somewhere to cook meals.

I bought a small range which burnt coal and had a little oven.

Joe and Peter fixed it and whitewashed the walls of the building inside. I got two camp beds, a table and two chairs, so all was ready for the boarders to take possession.

Never will I forget the look on their faces when I drove over to the camp to collect them. I signed two receipts, the first for Joe which read: 'Today April 1945 I have received the live body of Guissippe Claridi, the other one for the live body of Pedro Pedaline.'

'Thank you, boss, me very happy,' Joe said.

I was pleased to have the men on the farm to help with the planting and haymaking after tea-time.

We lived quite near and every Friday Joyce and I bought the rations for the prisoners from Evesham. 'Plenty macaroni and plenty tinned beans if you please, boss.' They grew tomatoes in a garden near where they lived.

'Potato friete very nice,' Joe would say as at evening I saw him stirring potatoes, tomatoes, margarine, beans in a pan on the range. Eggs they liked, but never bothered much about meat.

And like the men at Partridge Farm, Friday night was bath night. Powdered and scented, with Joe's black hair plastered straight back, they came as clean as two pins from their bath.

Speculation about Flick's association with Sebastian was a diversion from the milking and muck spreading for Charles Stephenson, Walt Gillet and Bill Brown.

''Tis what they calls fraternisation on the wireless and in the *Daily Herald*,' Charles declared over his midday lunch in the fields.

'They tells me as the Hittalions be past masters at making love,' Walt added.

Charles said between mouthfuls of bread and cheese that, 'I beunt one to pry, as you chaps know, but that Sebastian chap a got young Flick twisted round his little finger, summat of a Casanova.'

'Who the 'ell was he?' Walt replied. 'It sounds like some sort a tater.'

'Catriona thee bist thinking on, a early potato from Scotland.' Charles laughed as he explained that he understood a 'Casanova was a man with a eye for the women. A man they couldn't resist, different to country clodhoppers like thee and me, slick tongued they be and forrad.'

Bill Brown, who unbeknown to his workmates had been

more than once to the Dog and Muffler along with Audrey, had himself been to the local grammar school, he had learnt quite a lot of the world outside Ashton, learnt it from men of letters, not wireless and paper talk. 'Have you chaps ever heard about platonic friendship?' he said to his workmates.

'Sounds like summat from the next world,' Charles said.

'What dost thee think, Walt?'

Walt lit his clay pipe, spat with his usual accuracy into the fire on the headland, then said, 'I knows what you myuns, 'tis love avout sek.'

'Right,' said Bill, 'that can happen and that's what I think does happen between Flick and Sebastian.'

'That's as maybe,' Charles answered, 'but what about our bailiff and Audrey and their trip to Lunnon, theur gin and it at the Dog and Muffler, dost reckon that's plutonic or what you calls it, 'cause young Audrey, her's hot assed.'

Bill looked at his watch, then at the two older men saying, 'Come on, chaps, back to work, you can't do too much for a good master.'

Meanwhile down the road at my place Joe and Peter had settled in nicely. Peter built my corn ricks, then after about a two-hour lesson from Eric's dad he thatched them. They were indeed a credit to any rickyard, and Joe seemed to get stronger each day.

Three ricks near the main road were left until spring to thresh. Joe handled the two hundredweight and a quarter sacks of wheat as if they were twenty-pound nets of sprouts.

We were one man short for threshing, a man to carry away the rowans or cavings, the broken straw from under the threshing machine. Being April this was not needed to feed the cattle so I decided to burn it in the field.

A tramp slept in my old shed and asked for a job with the threshing gang.

I told him to carry the rowans a hundred yards away in a sacking sheet. He obliged, and the work went well apart from the dust.

After four days the ricks were almost finished and the old tramp did as I said, burnt the rowans. Dinner-time came when I took the men and girls back to the yard for an hour's break for a meal.

At about 1.30 a neighbour called telling me that all the straw ricks and the sacks of wheat were ablaze in the Thurness field.

I suppose my Wolseley Hornet car converted to a half-ton lorry never went so fast as I flew it over the station bridge to the threshing scene with half a mouthful of dinner still to swallow.

The heat was intense. Joe and Peter had burnt their shirts trying to save the sacked corn. Eric was using every ounce of strength to pull the sacks clear.

Harry, the engine driver, saved his tractor just in time, but my neighbour's almost-new Ransome threshing machine was but a skeleton of iron, all the woodwork burnt away.

The wind fanned the burning straw ricks as I dived in to try and rescue more sacks of corn. I was unsuccessful. The Land Girls were helpless too.

The Fire Brigade arrived but we had no water except the tankful they brought with them.

Yes, nearly a total loss, though we did save a nearby clover rick.

At tea-time when Joe, Peter, Eric, Tom Wheatcroft and Skemer washed under the water tap over the cattle trough, the smell of hair burnt from their arms was like that of the burning of a pig from the pig bench.

They had tried but tried in vain.

It was soon discovered that the cause of the fire was the tramp who dragged quite unwittingly a smouldering chaff sheet back to the ricks at dinner-time and threw it near the straw.

P.C. Woods came that evening. I remember his words so well, I remember them with regret. Regret at the smallness of a man's mind.

He said, 'Of course it's the Ities, you realise that?'

'Doubtful, very doubtful you would think, had you been here and seen them getting burnt trying to save my wheat. No, it's not the prisoners who started the fire.' I was adamant.

'Now look here, Mr. Archer,' he said, 'It's up to you to start the ball rolling and we will have the enemy punished as they should be. Come with me and look at the burnt-out machine.'

I went.

'Look for a cigarette with two match sticks tied to it with cotton.'

'But why?' I said.

'That's how they start fires. A lighted cigarette smoulders until it reaches the brimstone on the matches, then come the flames. Prisoners do this,' he added.

'Not mine wouldn't,' I said, walking away.

Someone told Peter and Joe that P.C. Woods had them under suspicion. They both came to my back door, Joe was the spokesman.

'Boss,' he said, 'do you want us to go back to camp, me no like some people talk about us and the fire.'

'Joe, you stay. I know you tried to save my wheat not to burn it. This is my business and I am satisfied with you.'

'Some people, boss, make me feel very sick,' Joe said. 'Thank you, boss, we stay with you.'

Some Sundays Joe and Peter, who by now had made themselves bicycles out of parts from cast-off machines of the villagers, rode back to the camp to watch their fellow prisoners play football.

I spoke to Joe about this and asked why a strong fit man like himself did not play.

'Boss, me no play because if me break my leg Mr. Churchill will not give me another one and, boss, when me dead me always dead, six feet in ground finish Joseph.'

'No finish,' I said to him. 'You live again.'

'Boss, you similar the Pope him say that, you mistake, boss.'

I looked at Joseph, his hair brushed back, his face had a sallow Romany look.

'I have not a brother,' he said with some feeling. 'My mother now she is old, not possible for her to make another Joseph. You Englisese very good to me, but I wish to see my mother.'

Joe walked away. Later I found that he had written on the stable door these words:

'To love and not to be loved is time wasted'. I wonder did Joe love someone.

Peter soon found in our village a Polly Garter of a girl, Cynthia Strange. After work in the evening he met her on the railway bridge and together they walked to an old cowshed on the edge of the cricket field.

Cynthia was about seventeen, worked for a market gardener, dyed her hair auburn and had hung around the American army camp, walking the hill with some homesick G.I. I knew her as a child, a baby of a girl of nine who lay on her mother's lap at Chapel asleep long before the last hymn. She was what we would have called a bit gaumless.

The youngest of the family, she was now away from her mother's apron strings, cutting quite a dash with any chap in uniform.

'Boss, me very jealous of Peter who has Cynthia for company,' Joe said sadly. 'You think right, prisoner go with girl from this village?'

I smiled, knowing Cynthia just had to have a man whoever he was. The evening meetings were regular. Every night Peter shaved again and spruced himself up for Cynthia.

Peter came to me one Friday and said, 'Boss, you go Evesham today?'

'Yes I always go on a Friday. What do you want, more macaroni, spaghetti?'

Joe winked and laughed, 'I think something different, boss.'
'What is it?'

Peter looked me straight in the eye and said, 'I want to take precautions, I fear about Cynthia if she became pregnant.'

'I'll think about that,' I said, but as I drove to town that afternoon I thought Cynthia is a simple stupid girl and if she has a child it will be a tragedy.

At a herbalist in town known as the Prevention Officer I rightly or wrongly bought for Peter what are advertised as surgical goods.

On my way to Chapel one Sunday I met a villager and walked with him and we talked of the prisoners.

He said, 'I understand your prisoner Peter is keeping company with Cynthia Strange and I understand he is a married man.'

'Yes, that's true, he was but he has not heard from home for some years.'

'I think you should put a stop to this association,' he said.

'What Peter does after work is not my business,' I answered. 'He works well for me in the day, who am I to dictate morals to him.'

My friend said no more and I have thought since it was a delicate question. Cynthia's welfare was important, but two years went by and she was never in the family way although Joe said she was like a threshing machine whose only tune was more, more, more.

So the little colony of Mussolini's army settled in the village. Feelings were mixed, one can understand why. You see, the local farmers in the main treated these men fairly, they lived on reasonable rations while across the water in Hitler's Germany some of our lads had a very rough time. The camps were crowded, some of the Nazi guards were bullies. In general there is kindness in the English. It shows in their treatment of animals. It was shown also to prisoners of war.

'Finish carboni,' Joe announced one morning. 'Not possible to cook some potato frieti.'

I sent Eric to Beckford with the pony and dray to fetch the ration of coal, about five hundredweight.

Eric was always pulling Joe's leg; he had a way with him and could speak Italian quite well.

Back in the yard so that he could be overheard by Joe he said, 'The coalman asked me, Fred, whether the coal was for you or them blasted Ities. I said the Italian prisoners. "Go to the next truck, Eric, the coal in there is good enough for prisoners." So I bought some cheaper coal.'

I nodded and smiled, knowing that this was a leg pull and that our coalman only had one grade of coal. I looked at the invoice and found this was so.

Joe threw his arms in the air. He called on Christ and Mary, he kept repeating that 'Anythink will do for those blasted prisoners'.

Peter laughed, knowing that the whole thing was a joke.

Joe was so emotional yet kind.

One Saturday when he was short of bread he almost wept; another day, twice in fact, Dad fell against the pig swill boiler as he cooked potatoes for his pigs. Weak and unsteady on his legs he would have been burnt to death but Joe ran and carried him away from the red-hot boiler.

'I tell you something, boss,' he said to me. 'If your father was as strong on his legs as he is in his arms he would be a strong man. I see him, boss, swinging the axe to split the wood for the fire.'

The weeks, the months, even the years went by. Life was so different on the land when even the cart horses laid their ears and fidgeted when a party of those Tom Wheatcroft described as Chanoos were chattering around to each other in the harvest field. It's strange how horses know the sound of the British labourers' leisurely speech. The 'Gee Baak', 'Cummey Baak' falls lightly on their ears.

The Italians were cute with the little money they had. They caught rabbits in snares on the hill which they bartered between themselves for shillings. Shillings to file into fancy chased rings for the village girls, for Cynthia and her friends.

When the war finished with the Nazi Fascist forces Joe grew uneasy for his native land. A letter telling him of the death of his father made him more anxious to see his mother again.

'Boss, when me return to Italy? War finis now.'

I said, 'Plenty British prisoners not yet return to England.' Joe just sighed. He had saved some money which he used to buy a barrel of cider. He and Peter drank after their meal in the evening. Something in the fermented apple juice promoted them to sing together the songs of their homeland.

'Very nice English cider, it make us happy for a little while, boss,' they told me.

I am convinced without doubt that by giving my prisoners a measure of liberty more work was done by Peter and Joe than was achieved by the few bullying, shouting, swearing employers whose methods were so futile. You see, I could go to the market with either cattle or fruit and vegetables and be away half a day, knowing full well that as much work would be done as if I was on the farm.

I know this has always applied to the majority of British farm workers who are and have been the salt of the earth.

There is a sort of gentleman's agreement between the farmer and his men that if the weather is bad the men put in their time at clearing up jobs around the buildings, unprofitable as this may seem.

On the other hand in good weather when crops are fit to harvest or carry, every man from the farmer himself to the boy who sometimes leans against the stable door post pulls his weight. They go that extra mile. Saturday nights when the weather has been fine we have loaded every waggon with hay, making sure of a pleasing sight in the rickyard when the hay is safe from the weekend storm.

There is no doubt that this give-and-take' on the land has been the reason for good relations between master and men.

Men do appreciate seeing the boss take off his jacket and work together with them.

When the time was near for Joe and Peter to go back to Naples Joe often said to me, so quietly, so kindly but with a touch of mischief, 'Boss, you been married over a year, Joyce not yet got a bambino. You start a family, boss, because people of Ashton-under-Hill will speak you no good.'

One March morning a furniture van arrived to take away the 'two live bodies' I had signed for at the camp, of Pedro Pedaline and Guissippe Claridi. As Joe climbed onto the tail with his few belongings I said, 'Joe, I have news for you, Joyce will have a bambino at the end of the summer.'

He and Peter gripped my hand as they left and said just two words, 'Thank you.'

As the van went around the corner full of singing Italians, Joe shouted, 'Cheerio Ashton-under-Hill.'

Some of our lads came back about that time from Germany. They had had a rough time in the prison camps living on raw turnips or anything to keep them alive. Germany was hungry and broken and with it some of our men were broken too.

So the difference is apparent. To be a prisoner of war is bad for any man. To be a prisoner of war in England was bearable. As I said before we treat our prisoners as we do our animals, with humanity.

12

The Last of the Waggoners

ERIC PACKER WAS A HANDY LAD ON THE FORDSON
tractor. He'd change gear without using the clutch. His hearing
was so acute something told him the split second when the
lever on the gearbox could be slid from second to third gear.
Mind you, he didn't make a practice of this, but he showed
me how it could be done.

Early mornings when the oil in the gearbox was thick and
gluey after a freezing night, when neighbours' Fordsons were
being forced into gear to the accompaniment of arguing cogs
in the gearbox, and the gnashing, as we called it, could be

heard a quarter of a mile away, Eric engaged his tractor into gear without a murmur.

It was a pity that I was unable to get some pneumatic-tyred wheels for Eric's tractor. The spade lugs we had gripped the ground and marked the turf at haymaking, but when it came to hauling the loads of hay and corn three-quarters of a mile into my rickyard, the horses and broadwheeled waggons rumbled up the Station Road. Fanshaw, Bennet's bailiff, with Bert Amos just changed the wheels on his tractor from spade lugs of iron to pneumatic. Bennet could get anything, while we remained in a long queue for things in short supply.

Mr. Higgins, the Sedgeberrow blacksmith, was busy making trailers from old lorry bodies for the tractors to pull, but this was useless to me because the iron wheels were not allowed on council roads.

Dick, who had just left school, was working for me and was handy in the hayfield, raking with Tom the cob, loading the waggons. He was a strong lad for his age and relieved Tom Wheatcroft with the cattle feeding and calf suckling at haymaking time. Dick came from a long line of Evesham market gardeners; his grandfather had always been a master man with a few acres of fruit. But Dick was not old enough nor experienced enough to haul great loads of hay across the main road, where the American convoys knocked over the paint pots for the white lines to annoy the local roadman, and their drivers threw chocolate to the Land Girls and sweets to the children.

Then there was a further hazard between the Thurness field and our rickyard where thirty loads of hay had to be taken by the waggons—a steep, slippery railway bridge, the surface of which was ideal for motor traffic but bad for horses' shiny shoes.

A time comes in life when between thirteen and eighteen birthdays have dawned, a time when youth becomes impatient.

'Hobbledehoys,' Tom Wheatcroft called the potential house-holders of the village.

'Ah,' he sighed, 'they be neither a man nor a boy.'

Eric was at that stage when he drove my waggons up and down the Station Road. He was fearless with horses, perhaps wasted a little on my staid teams, Pleasant, Prince and Bounce, when I'm sure he would have handled some spirit-filled three-year-olds.

The important thing was that the heavy-laden waggons got home to the rickyard.

I watched Eric across the main road as Prince, the trace horse, pulled his full weight and knew that he had to cross that slippery tarmac while Pleasant in the shafts came straight through the rutted gateway from the field.

A pull on the leading rein from Eric who still used the language of his father, a man who had worked with horses when the old Queen Vic was still on the throne.

'Cummy back,' Eric called to Prince as he lightened the leather rein which was buckled to Prince's crupper above his tail while the other end fastened by a spring clipped hook to the ring on the bit. The bit on the mullen or bridle was still green from the new-mown hay he had snatched in the field while the waggon was loaded.

Prince stepped out smartly along that three hundred yards of main road until the loaded waggons were near the foot of the bridge.

'Whoo!' shouted Eric. The waggon stopped, its waggoner lit a Woodbine, looked at the roped load and had what we called a blow.

Once more the challenge came to man and beast to reach safely the crest of the hill.

'Cup Prince, come on, Pleasant,' and the mare and her son broke into a fast trot.

The iron tyres of the waggon rattled on the road. The dry spokes of the wheels creaked while a ton of hay was pulled by two horse power to the top of Station Bridge.

So often Harry White the railway ganger dropped his sledge hammer and ran to the bridge as the noise of hooves' metal, the thunder of the waggons echoed on the bridge.

Harry was Eric's uncle, near retirement, good at his work but a bundle of nerves.

'Bless the boy,' he would shout, 'you'll be the death of me, can't you come up the bank steady?'

But Eric knew that without a flying start the horses might have stopped halfway. Then the scaut or scotch (a wedge of wood carried at the back of the waggon) might have stopped it running back if it was put behind the rear wheel.

This never happened; with Eric always with his right hand on the waggon shaft end to help him along and his left holding the leading rein, my team made the bridge incline.

At the top the horses stopped. Pleasant held the load back as the breeching strap tightened across what Tom always called her ass part and Eric put the lock chain on the near side hind wheel with the heavy skid pan just in front of the tyre. As the team moved on, this wheel turned until the chain was tight, and the skid pan lay like a heavy iron shoe. Sliding over the tarmac it soon became hot. Not an unpleasant smell, the fumes from sizzling tar rising like steam off a boiling kettle when a locked wheel glided down the bridge.

Tom Wheatcroft, another uncle of Eric's, was a handy man around horses, his eye seemed continually on the tackle. A glance to see whether the traces were level on the chain horse.

Then he knew by an uncanny instinct how well or badly the collar fitted, running his hand under the checked lining, observing the sweat line on the horses' shoulders, always looking for sore or rubbed places, telling me when the collars needed relining at Ernie Hines, the Saddler's. We were advised by Tom to take a fleece of sheep's wool to the saddler's and ask him to use it with the straw to make a softer collar lining.

'When you only got three hosses, Eric bwoy, you can't afford to have one with sore shoulders or crupper galls, nor a lame animal when we be busy.'

We agreed.

Under the rick when we drank hot tea with shirts wet through with sweat, Tom told us, 'It unt like the last war mind.'

Skemer sucked his breath as if the temperature was zero, turned to me and said, 'Thee dosn't remember 1917, dost, Fred?'

I shook my head.

'That was a cold spring when the telegraph wires was fetched down along the railroad, Oi, in April and all.'

Tom was thinking of other happenings in 1917.

'Oi, that's right, Skemer, but what I myuns is that in that war any useful hoss on the farm was drafted to France to pull the guns. Oi, just when they was useful.'

'Did you lose any, Tom?' I said.

Tom didn't answer straightaway. Staring as if into the past he recalled how that, many a night he had gone to bed wet-eyed after the Military had culled all the best young hosses off Freddy Counsell's farm.

Skemer sucked his breath, Eric looked at me, and we smiled not because of horses going into the army, but at Skemer's face.

'Oi, they fetched mine out of a coal dray, and left me with a one-eyed mare. Still, this lot ull soon be over, just wait until Russia starts.'

Yes, Skemer was optimistic.

After Eric had hauled the last load of corn to the rickyard some weeks after the hay was in, Henry Fanshaw on a brand-new Fordson on rubber tyres was hauling potatoes fresh lifted off the hill. No end of a fellow was Henry with his smart breeches, gaiters and canary yellow gloves.

The loads got heavier as more and more sacks were loaded into his pneumatic-tyred trailer.

'Put the brake on,' Bert Amos said, 'when you go down the Nap.'

But Henry sat on his tractor so confident. The look on his face was as much as to say 'I'll show these country chaps a thing or two'. He said that man's pace was geared to the plod of the plough horse.

At the Nap the load pushed the tractor until the trailer was at right angles. Henry jumped clear as the tractor careered down the hill hitting an ash tree and bursting its radiator.

When Tom Wheatcroft heard this in the Dog and Muffler pub he smiled as Henry said that his trailer jack-knifed.

'Now look yer, Master Fanshaw, young Eric has got all our crops home without as much as hitting a gate post. Now you was warned by Bert to put the brake on, so thurs only yourself to blame.'

That harvest season was the last for Prince and Pleasant to haul the loads. I bought a second-hand pair of pneumatic tyres (rather bald) at a farm sale and Eric brought home the loads on the waggons with a tow bar in place of the shafts.

So Eric was the last of a long line of horsemen who had brought in the harvest. Our mare Bounce went lame and injured her back, and I suppose I felt a bit like Tom Wheatcroft as the horse slaughterer dropped her to the ground with his humane killer.

To say cart horses are faithful is an understatement. They worked for me among the flies of July and the sleet of January.

Young Dick worked Prince and Pleasant on the harrows and roller, in the four-wheeled dray hauling the vegetables to the station, but the thunder of Eric's horsedrawn waggon over our Railway Bridge is pleasant to recall.

Just a thought that Grandad helped to build the bridge and the four-foot way for the railway to open in 1864.

Then Dad crossed it so often with donkey and cart thirty years later. Now as I write it's just been taken down, only a hump in the road marks the place. The line's been closed.

13

Meeting Sammy's Brother

ALTHOUGH WE PLOUGHED MOST OF THE LEVEL LAND
in our village I had some sloping hill pasture fit only for raising
store cattle.

Tom Wheatcroft and I were still busy rearing the red and
white Hereford calves I bought from Gloucester market. I
used a part of my petrol ration those Saturday mornings to go to
the market while Joyce queued for the few items of food which
were unobtainable in our town of Evesham.

Gloucester market in the city centre was a sort of Mecca to
me. I had seen cheapjacks selling crockery, the horse copers

running their Shires with feathered fetlocks which draped their hooves like sills up and down outside the Spread Eagle. Horsy men with bowler hats and whips were few now. Henry Ford's tractor tore through the turf in Gloucestershire and Worcestershire.

The auctioneer in the cattle ring gave us an entertainment difficult to describe. Confronted by dealers in milk cows and calves he held his own, keeping up a continuous patter of talk in competition with bawling cows and calves and the shouting of lorry drivers, farmers and the man in a reddle-stained smock with an ash stick who beat the beasts as they unwillingly entered the ring.

The dealers squeezed streams of milk from the bloated udders of newly-calved cows.

When a cow lifted her leg to kick the dealers shouted, 'She's a kicker.'

At this point the farmer would enter the ring and milk the cow, a drop from each of her four quarters, and Daisy or Dot stood back, knowing the familiar touch of its owner.

'How much? Start me reasonable,' the auctioneer called out as he leant over the rostrum with his gavel at the ready.

'Thirty pound,' one dealer called as he ran his hand along the cow's back.

'If Brown offers thirty, she's worth forty,' the auctioneer said, looking for another bid.

'All right thirty-five,' Brown bid, and the figure rose in five shillings and ten shillings until forty was reached, the wooden hammer-like gavel hit the rostrum front as the clerk took Brown's name and the word 'Sold' echoed through the corrugated iron building.

Next lot, a heifer and her calf, was announced. Brown and Jackson opened her mouth, protesting to the rostrum that 'She's no heifer but a long-toothed old cow'.

I smiled as the old bag of bones followed by her calf circled the ring like an old man recovering from 'flu.

'A heifer and her calf I have here, and she may well be,' our auctioneer declared with a wry smile, adding 'perhaps she was married very late in life'.

My Friesian cross came next, a second calver, but I was keeping the calf. Eric's friend Alf had travelled with her in the cattle truck and was as anxious as me to get a good price.

'Are you bidding?' the auctioneer bellowed at Alf.

'No,' Alf replied.

'Well, don't look at me then,' the answer came.

I wonder did Alf put a pound or two on my cow. Anyhow, she was sold, and Alf and I brought the calf home in the back of my 1934 Austin-ten tourer.

Alf was sitting in the back holding the halter.

'Forty-two pounds she made, Alf,' I said. 'How about if you had have bought her when you looked at the rostrum?'

'Daresay I could have paid.'

Before we started for home Alf and I had a wartime snack in the British Restaurant, dried egg and potato and jelly like rubber. There we met Sammy Bosworth from Minsterworth, and his brother Archie who had moved to the river meadows when the ploughing-up campaign got under way. He liked cows and hated corn growing, but he had just experienced his first flood as the Severn Bore swept up from the Bristol Channel to the narrow waters of the Severn in Gloucestershire.

The high wave was timed for early morning in the spring. Farmers moved stock to higher ground from the flood-threatened meadows.

This year the Bore tide was higher than ever. A mammoth wave drove up the narrow river, bursting its banks, covering hedges, gates, willow trees, drowning rabbits before they could climb the taller withies to safety and lifting ailing sheep to a watery grave down the Severn.

Archie told me as he smoked his pipe over his spam sandwich how the force of water had lifted all his farm gates from their hinges and taken them Bristol road on the ebb tide.

'I be coming up to Aysham,' he said, 'to get the old hurdle

maker to make some gates to keep my cows in. There are no gates for sale at the merchants'.'

I nodded, Sam nodded, knowing that our hurdle maker had slept west of our church tower these three years or more.

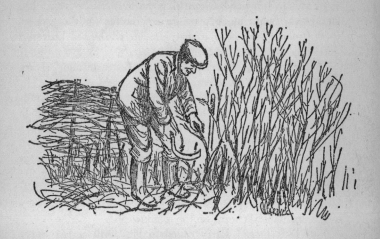

14

No Bull

IT JUST DOESN'T SOUND RIGHT FOR THE GRASSY
acres of Bredon Hill, where the cattle fed all the summer and
were yarded after Christmas, not to have a bull.

During the war Thomas Bennet bought a red Shorthorn bull
from Reading.

Despite footpaths, bridlepaths, public rights of way, Stanley
the bull ran the field with the milk cows and heifers.

When Jim Hicks spoke to Henry about this risk, Henry just
drove his hands deep into his breeches pockets, rattled the little
silver he had, and replied,

'Damn it, Jim, don't you know there's a war on.'

Jim looked at Bennet's bailiff, a look which had sixty-odd years of knowledge of Bredon Hill country.

'So thur might be, but we be responsible for the vacuees from Brumingham. Now if that spiteful red-skinned little sod gores one, what then?' he replied.

'Nonsense, Jim, Stanley's all right, no harm in him,' Henry said, shrugging his shoulders.

Sometime after Bennet's cows were turned up near the railway line where Harry White was cropping the hedge beside the track. Stanley was out of work that day as none of Bennet's cows were on bulling.

He walked with the jerky walk of a mischievous bull towards the hedge. Harry was swinging his hedge hook, clipping the top shoots of hawthorn level as railway hedges were. Every blow with the hook at the springy hedge was countered by a butt from Stanley's horns on the meadow side.

'Get back there,' Harry called to him until at last Harry walked up the line and started work on another length of hedge.

Stanley followed with tail erect. He stalked Harry up and down the hedge with just the hawthorn between the bull's horns and Harry.

The bull was moved to another field with some heifers. He broke the fence, spending the night up and down the village street bellowing like a bull elephant.

The evacuees couldn't go to school until he was persuaded into the yard at Partridge Farm.

'We'll have to keep him tied up,' Bert Amos said.

'Oi,' Charles Stephenson remarked. 'Funny things be bulls, they beunt to be trusted.'

Standing up to his manger the Shorthorn looked around, rattling his tie chain while Charles stroked his back.

'Now Herefords be different, most in general they be as quiet as an old sheep. Ther's the hexceptional a course, like some young fellas—a couple of pints of cider and they ull threaten to fight the best man around; but this yer joker, I udn't trust him no farther than I could spit. Just look at his eyes, thurs the devil for ya.'

Henry Fanshaw strode across the yard from his breakfast at Rosemary Cottage. 'Twenty heifers this bull has to serve and he's not safe now to turn out. I have an idea,' he continued. 'When I was at college vets were experimenting with some injection to make the heifers come on bulling.'

Walt Gillet stood and listened, suggesting that the best way was to bring the heifers up from the fields when they were bulling and turn the bull in the yard with them every day one was ready.

'Time wasting man hours, driving awkward cattle to and from,' Henry replied.

'What's this yer nejection?' Charles raised his eyebrows, adding, 'It unt nature ya know.'

'We will see. Bert, you and Charles fetch the heifers now into the yard and I'll ring the vet.'

The vet said he would give the injection but was dubious whether it was wise to do them all on the same day. As the heifers were gated tight in the stable the vet injected them.

Some days later, when Charles Stephenson was making his morning walk to count the cattle he came into the yard breathless.

'What's the matter, Charles?' Bert asked him. 'Are the cattle on the railroad?'

'No, the damn lot be on a bulling. They be riding each other around the field like a rodeo.'

Bert fetched Henry. Henry was a little amused.

'It's worked then,' he said. 'Fetch them all up into the yard.'

As they circled the stone paved enclosure Stanley sensed something. He tugged on his chain bellowing and snorting.

'Loose him, Bert,' Henry said.

''Alf a minute, gaffer.' Charles walked towards the bailiff carrying his ash plant stick.

'One heifer at a time don't you reckon is more feasible for the bull to see to?'

'Loose the bull, Bert,' Henry shouted in annoyance.

Stanley met the herd and, with tail erect and snorting nostrils, made his way between them.

Trying to mount and serve the first, another heifer feeling in the same mood knocked the young bull off. This happened time and time again as every heifer tried its utmost to make love at the same time to one young bull.

Charles sat on the fence and puffed at his pipe.

'I'll tell tha what, Walt,' he said. 'This job ull spoil him like enough, he'll be what they calls frustrated and lose all interest in heifers.'

After about two hours of wasted time Stanley was tied up again, his red back covered with muck, his ribs moving like bellows from sheer exhaustion.

The heifers were returned unserved to the field.

Some time after I bought a Hereford bull at the market. He was, I suppose, about eleven months old, a bit short in the legs. Our cows were a mixed lot, used for calf rearing. They were tall. Some of the Friesians were animals which had calved five or six times. The bull served several of Bennet's heifers when Bert and Charles brought them down to my yard.

'Useful animal,' Charles said. 'Not too much daylight under him, stocky, unt he?'

I agreed.

The time came when Darkie, my biggest cow, was a bulling; the Hereford mounted, but was much too short to reach the cow and serve.

'Tell tha what,' Skemer suggested, 'let's lead him by his nose ring up on to the top of that muck bury.'

Skemer led the bull. I held Darkie on a halter and Tom nosed her, that is, he put the bulldogs or nose clips in his nose, and we backed her against the heap of muck. The Hereford mounted.

'Capital job,' Skemer said, as he winked at Tom and me.

'Now next year things ull be different, that husband beast ull be tall enough to serve the cows without that caper.'

So we lived and learnt even from Skemer, who looked so

pleased as he sucked his breath through those ill-fitting, butter-coloured false teeth of his.

But Tom told me after that it didn't pay me to keep a bull for my few cows and the ones that came when the owners paid me ten shillings a time, and for what was often quite a long business.

Skemer explained that Herefords take their time. 'They be like some folk, they wants to play about a bit.'

'Skemer,' I said, 'I'll tell your missus that.'

'No, don't thee dare to, Fred,' he answered. 'Her won't speak to me agun for a month else.'

We liked to tease Skemer, but that finished at the yard gate.

When Eric's tractor was slow to start if a plug was oiled up, Eric would lay the plugs on top of the cylinder head and turn the starting handle while I watched for the spark as the plugs fired in turn.

'Which one is it?' Eric asked me. 'It's usually the one at the back which doesn't fire.'

'I'll tell that,' Skemer said. 'Let me hold um two at a time.'

The impulse starter on the magneto sent a strong current through the plugs on the first turn of the starting handle. As the electricity shot up old Skemer's arms they just twitched.

'They be all right, now let's hold the t'others,' he said, and sure enough Skemer told us which plug was misfiring.

'I never met another man who would do that,' said Eric, and we laughed, knowing full well that we wouldn't try.

Skemer had driven a Model T Ford in his younger days, delivering coal.

'Oi, the lorry stopped one day up the Poplar Row and our gaffer didn't know what to do. All I did,' he said, 'was to get a bit of barbed wire out of the hedge and join the main plug to the ignition and away we went.'

Not even to this day do we know what he did, but that was his tale to us.

Anyway, I sold the bull when the Artificial Insemination

Centre started. I was the first in the village to have cows served this way. It caused a deal of talk and speculation.

The A.I. man arrived in his van one morning after I'd 'phoned for him. He was more like a salesman selling seed corn.

In his bag he had the different glass containers marked Hereford, Friesian, Shorthorn, Devon, Jersey, Ayrshire and the lot.

We gathered around, Tom Wheatcroft, Eric, Skemer, Dick and me.

The cow was chained. I fetched a bucket of hot water, some soap, a towel, and the A.I. man took off his coat and put on an oilskin overall.

He rolled up his sleeves, washed his hands in the bucket, then put on a pair of rubber gloves which reached his elbows.

'What breed do you want, Mr. Archer?' he said.

'Oh Hereford,' I answered.

He took a glossy catalogue of some fine Hereford animals.

'I think we will try that one, number 74.'

With this he filled a glass tube with semen from a bottle.

Skemer raised his eyebrows, gave an extra suck between his teeth.

'Just hold her nose,' the A.I. man asked Eric, and we stood at the tail end.

With one arm up her back passage he cleared away some cow dung and steered the glass tube, which he inserted where the bull should plant the seed.

One injection and it was over; he washed himself and his tube and was ready to go.

'This 'udn't a done in the Squire's time,' Skemer said to Tom. 'Dost remember all the bulls he had at the Manor when we worked there? A big white un there was, savage as a tup. He was never let loose, Oi, ten years old if he was a day.'

The A.I. man then tried to explain to us how the semen or seed was diluted with egg yolk and that the amount obtained from one ejaculation of the bull was enough to serve dozens of cows.

'It's against nature,' Tom said, 'and anyway, how do you get the seed?'

'This is Tom Wheatcroft, my stockman,' I explained. 'He's been handling cattle since long before we were born.'

'Now, Mr. Wheatcroft, we get the semen in several ways. One way is to put a cow in a crush or small stall, one that's on a bulling. The bull jumps to serve her and we slip a rubber sheath on his penis. These bulls are worth more than Mr. Archer would want to pay.'

Skemer laughed, saying, 'Summat like the Yank uses.'

I looked at Skemer and said, 'Shall I tell your missus?'

He looked in the A.I. man's bag at what he called the samples.

Tom turned to me and said, 'How about the Land Girls? I hope they aren't around here, it's not a fit place for women. You know how particular we were when we had a cow bulled in the proper way.'

I assured him that the girls were in the fields, far enough away.

'Of course I could have come tomorrow,' the A.I. man said, 'that would have been all right.'

'All right,' said Tom. 'Bless the fella, the cow would be gone off bulling by then. A bull wouldn't look at her tomorrow and don't tell me that a bull can't tell when a cow's what we call beasting.'

'This is the difference,' and holding the glass tube towards us, he said, 'I put this tube into the cow much farther than the bull penetrates.'

Skemer looked really angry that this fella was being so sure of himself.

'Thee go and show thee granny how to suck eggs, I says, because I knows damn well a bull's tool is longer than that there tube.'

'That's what we are told at the Centre where we train,' he answered Skemer.

A couple of weeks after, I met a neighbouring farmer in the

market, one of the old school of men who had handled stock all his life.

'Do you have your cows served by artificial insemination?' he asked me.

'Yes, I've had two or three done.'

'I had one done yesterday and I don't think she enjoyed it very much,' he said with a laugh.

So Ashton became a village without a bull, and Tom Wheatcroft summed it up well when he said, 'Very soon the only bull there will be ull be in the army.'

15

It Took a War

'FUNNY THING, IT TOOK A WAR TO MAKE OUR gaffer clean out his ditches,' Jim Hicks told Skemer as my man, who always had to 'Ask the Missus', made his half pint last until someone offered to buy him another one at the Dog and Muffler.

Skemer sucked and showed what Eric called his ivories once more.

'That's the War Ag., unt it?' he answered.

'You must admit that they have done some good up at No Gains Farm. Sammy Bosworth's land lies much drier than before the main ditch which emptied into Currants Brook was running free, cleaned out by the War Ag. machines.'

Old men who had shaken their heads and said 'It wouldn't have done in the Squire's time' saw permanent grass fields growing golden grain. There was an old idea among them that to plough certain fields was nothing short of sacrilege.

Good feeding pasture, they said, took a lifetime to make.

'These yer leys,' Jim said, 'be all right to look at, but the grass is nesh [tender], it goes through the cattle like a dose of salts.'

'Buttercups and cowslips don't make milk or beef,' the War Ag. said. They are weeds, so the fields which were not ploughed were sometimes sprayed, which spelt doom to the conservative Jim Hicks.

'Notice,' Jim told Sammy Bosworth, 'how the ewes graze the headland where the old herbages grows. On new pastures clover and grass look all right but the ewes find the need for what the War Ag. call weeds.'

Life is full of surprises especially on the land, where in peace-time the circle turns from scarcity of crops and fodder one year to gluts in the next.

It's true that fields once taken over by ant hills, rabbits and ragwort, when ploughed and fallowed so that the sun's rays could give life to the soil, then dressed with nitrogen, potash and phosphates, grew remarkable crops of corn.

I grew good potatoes and strawberries on such land.

Noticing the wild strawberries growing in the hedges, it struck me that this acid bit of Bredon Hill soil known as Fox Earth would grow strawberries for market.

I planted Huxley's Giant in April and twelve months the next July the plants were loaded with some of the finest fruit I'd seen. No fertiliser, just skim ploughed between the rows with a horse and hand hoed by the Italians. We had two tons off a small patch, but next year they beat us, as the runners joined up the rows, forming a mass of plants and small fruit.

As the War Ag. told me to grow ten acres of potatoes and

the Scotch seed was dear and large, the gamble on virgin soil was a bit frightening when it took more than a ton of seed to plant an acre.

Arthur, a neighbouring market gardener, said, 'Buy Scotch thirds or small seed.'

How many for ten acres, I thought? It was decided to order three tons. They came sound and clean, all one size like pigeons' eggs. My brother's tractor man bouted the field out with a little Allis Chalmers tractor and a three-furrow bouting out plough, a bouting out plough being a plough with two mould boards which makes channels to plant the crop in.

We started planting, filling out, two-gallon buckets with the small seed on the headland. There were Italians, Land Girls, Tom, Eric, Dick and myself.

Tom smiled at the seed and soon told me that I had bought enough to plant all Bredon Hill. Ten acres were planted and still there were a lot of sacks over, so we planted them in a wet field by the brook.

Those Majesties were true to their name, they yielded well, but those on the brook-side field just wouldn't cook. I sold these to members of the pig club for a few shillings a bag. The furnaces steamed hour after hour. The water boiled away and had to be topped up but these potatoes were as hard as when they went in the boiler. I'm afraid the pigs had to eat those under-done. Funny things, potatoes, they eat well off some land, not so well off others.

The fields, the yards, the orchards, the cottages and farm houses were now ringing with the voices of what Tom Wheat-croft described as 'People from away'.

As the Italians chattered and sang, the budding Carusos of the fields, the Land Girls from Bristol made us familiar with the expression 'Where ya to' and the 'hes' instead of him. The girls from Birmingham and the North Midlands, Dorothy in particular, spoke in a relaxed kind of drawl.

They also said 'basskit' while we said 'baaskeet'; they 'ashd' questions while we 'askhed' them questions.

Just thirty-six miles away a different brogue. Then Jim Hicks and Skemer still spoke as Shakespeare did with Thee's and Thou's.

It does make me think of the failure of the Old Testament folk to build the Tower of Babel. A tower to heaven because of language difficulty.

Among the hedgerows here the Italians sang, laughed and swore. The German Austrians all helped to harvest the corn and we seemed to understand each other.

While the girls from Yorkshire laughed at us and the London girls said 'ARR' 'ARR' as they mocked the folk of the Middle West.

The village children chewed gum like the Americans, thinking of them in their gaudy uniforms all as Hollywood film stars. Among all the strife abroad, here it was surprising how the cigarettes went round at lunch-time in the hedge bottom.

Exceptions? Why, of course, there is always the man or woman who thinks and acts differently. Just a few of the village folk would have willingly shot the Italians, sent the Land Girls back to where they belonged, but these folk were few, just ignorant, more to be pitied than blamed.

After all, this had been their patch of the earth's surface which had been scratched by their ancestors who lived off it for centuries.

So the war ended after nearly six years and we liked to think that the corn, the beef, the plums from our parish helped a little to feed the men who fought and the munition worker.

Every apple, even one an inch-and-a-half in diameter, regardless of its variety, was in demand at sixpence a pound.

Jim Hicks was surprised when Sammy Bosworth told him to pick the Bittersweets and some sort very like crab apples, because they were too big to go through the one-and-a-half-inch hole he had made in a piece of plywood to grade the fruit.

'As sour as Varges [Verjuice],' Jim said.

Sammy answered him with a quick retort that winter.

'At Michaelmas and a little afore, half the apple's thrown

away with the core. At Christmas or a little bit after, if it's as sour as a crab apple, it's thank you, master.'

'You see, Jim, nothing must be wasted when there is no foreign fruit.'

'It udn't be them sixpences you be after, Master Bosworth, ud it?' Jim replied.

Sammy let that statement slip and said nothing.

When V.E. Day came and our rations were pooled for a high tea, once more the bells rang again. It was good to hear them. The village made merry in the Church Close, our plasterer played the school piano perched on a tractor trailer. The village sang again, the children raced for the little prizes.

The Vesper at the Chapel had been changed at the beginning of the war, changed from 'Keep us safe this night secure from all our fears. May Angels guard us while we sleep till morning light appears!'

For over five years we sang, 'Oh hear us when we cry to thee, for those in peril on the sea.'

How helpless we had been when so much of our shipping was lost in those early years.

Soon after the war was over, our first daughter Shelagh was born, four o'clock one morning at Evesham Maternity Hospital. Now I felt really a married man when Joyce came home in a hired car with seven pounds of La La La to break the silence of the early morning hours.

My village has changed, but as the song says, 'There's no place like home.'

16

After the Bonfire

SOON AFTER V.J. DAY WHEN THE SECOND BONFIRE
had lit Bredon Hill, competing with the many fires across
Evesham Vale on the Cotswold Edge, a trickle of service men
returned home.

I saw the difference five years in a P.O.W. camp had made
to at least two men who had worked side by side with me on
the land in the thirties.

Arch was of a tougher nature, he weathered the storm of
life in a prisoner of war camp apparently well.

I knew the grit he had, his physical energy, but who knew

besides himself the mental torture life away from our hillside had meant? Yes, Arch was and is one of the bulldog breed, the best type of Englishman whose family has carved a living from these acres for generations.

Perce was never so strong in the arms, and who knows but he of the hunger, the cold, he endured near the Russian frontier.

I walked with Joyce down our village one hot Sunday afternoon and saw a young man in battledress sitting at the village cross. His face was drawn as he quietly said,

'Hello, Fred, how are ya?'

I looked again and again, then realised it was Perce.

'Good to see you, Perce. There were rumours you were dead.'

Perce gave a smile.

'Dead,' he said, and rolling up his sleeve he added, 'You see, nothing much left but bones.'

'Anything you want?' I inquired. 'Eggs perhaps.'

Perce shook his head and explained to me that since being almost famished and on a forced march in bad weather he was under the doctor and on a diet. Like a baby growing up, his stomach would only take a little food and often.

But he improved slowly, though he has to live with a delicate digestion even now.

'I've got my discharge,' he told me, 'and maybe I'll go back on the land for a while.'

This he did and drove a tractor for my brother.

I always liked Perce. His outlook stretched much farther than the Vale, Bredon and the Cotswolds, a great thinker, and I for one was pleased to have him back amongst us again.

Thomas Bennet, a kind of Birmingham Squire in our village all through the war, running his business in the city, farmed Partridge Farm quite well with the aid of Henry Fanshaw. Despite his mistakes in the beginning the whole hillside, where the orchards blossomed and fruited, had improved by the use of fertilisers and the pruning of Bert Amos.

Mr. Bennet planned a house with a drive on Bredon Hill,

he planned the restoration of the workers' cottages, the building of a Village Hall. When he died suddenly at a Board Meeting in Birmingham we were stunned.

No-one knew how long prices would be guaranteed. Lloyd George let us down after the last war, the older farmers said; never again would farming be the Cinderella of industry, the Government said.

I had an open mind about this but wondered when Partridge Farm was sold for the value of the house. All that fruit, with hundreds of acres of hillside land, went for a song.

Henry Fanshaw left, while a fruit grower from around the hill worked the land and had a few years of good prices for produce.

'Ah,' Jim Hicks said. 'Sometimes young hosses dies and old hosses be bound to.'

'He wasn't old,' Sammy replied. 'Not so old as me, but board meetings are trying places to be when money is discussed.'

'Money,' Jim Hicks said, "tis round and meant to go round. You looks after yours, Mister Bosworth.'

Sammy ignored the hint but turned to me asking me how much my lambs made at Honeybourne Sale.

'Well,' I said, evading the question, 'they were put in separate hurdled pens and I can't tell you the average price off-hand.'

Sammy had taken his to Beckford Market and got top price. Drinks all round at the hotel got Bill Brown and Walt Gillet drunk at Sammy's expense while Syd Freeman left Sammy there, driving the lorry home and Sammy walked.

'Unt it time these Ities went w'hom to Hitterly now our chaps be coming back to the land?' Skemer sucked these words through his teeth at lunch-time under the hedge out of Peter and Joe's earshot.

Joe gathered the gist of our conversation and said, 'Boss, me in Angleterra, the war finish in Japan, when me see my mother? Boss, why you no write to Mister Churchill?'

Joe always thought there was a direct line between this hillside village and Number 10.

They went back soon after in a furniture van to Southampton.

Skemer opened his eyes wider that morning and made more hissing noises through his false dentures as the Italians cried when they shook me by the hand and Skemer himself was moved in his peculiar way.

We were short of labour on the farms for a while. The lads who left the land before the war bought old cars or motor bikes with their gratuity and went to the factories which sprang up south of Birmingham.

17

A Village of Changes

IT WAS SAD IN SOME WAYS HOW SO-CALLED PEACE
returned to our little niche under the hill, folk had to adjust
their lives. The soldier from the front must have been eager to
return, expecting the old, close-knit village where he knew
everybody personally.

I had stayed on my 150 acres and had seen the changes
here.

I saw Thomas Bennet's dreams disappear as he left our scene
quicker than he came at the onset of the war. Men and girls
had married, Thomas was going to restore the old-world

cottages for these couples. If only he had lived, say, another ten years, life would have been simpler.

The prisoners left the land, the Land Girls left except Daphne, who married a tractor driver, Carol a draughtsman at the local factory, and Joyce who had married me. But, as in 1919, where were the homes for heroes to live in? Council workers were drafted to the cities to clear up the mess of enemy bombs, so our young couples had to wait for new houses to be built. Houses which had been planned in 1939 were still a pipe dream in 1946.

Skemer Hill, who had worked for me for years, was now an old man, a man whose face had weathered wind, rain and sunshine since the 1870s. He lived in his cottage, did his garden and as he sat on the stone slab covering the water stand pipe he had seen it all happening. Many's the time I've listened to his tale of our village in his youth.

'The bobby nor the school gaffer unt as strict as they used to be,' he said. 'These yer bwoys on their motor bikes keeps me awake after eleven at night. It udn't a done in the Squire's time, Fred.'

I nodded, and knew what was happening.

In Sammy Bosworth's barn a local dealer who, as Tom Wheatcroft said, could see farther than his nose end, had stacked motor bikes in scores side by side with cars in the adjoining dutch barn.

'He a salted um down a purpose to bring um out when things be scarce,' Skemer said.

As the men returned from all points of the globe and found nowhere to live a married life, they took rooms at Sammy's big house, at Joe Smith's house, and bought motor bikes to get to work.

'No more humping two hundredweight sacks of corn for me or getting wet picking sprouts,' some said.

The war had been won, but the young men who had left the land took jobs in the towns, roaring through our village morning and night on their motor bikes. Some bought cars out of

Sammy's barn, cars that had not been cranked with the starting handle for five or six years. Cars which cost more money than the day they left the factory new and polished.

It's so true that city life was changed as the rosebay willow herb grew where houses had been bombed. In our village where the one bomb fell away in the fields no material damage was done, but things were different.

Eric Parker and Tom Wheatcroft both stayed with me. Dick grew into a strongish chap and took over the cows from Tom, who was now semi retired, but still built and thatched my corn ricks and set the drill at planting time.

Corporal Rose, who had been so proud to be General Allenby's bodyguard at Jerusalem, lodged in an outhouse, cooked on a primus, helped to tidy the churchyard; then, as if he had lived to see the end of it all, died suddenly alone in his bothy. Another character went, a bit of the old village as well known as the village cross, 'passed over Jordan', as George Pitcher (strong Chapel) said.

So as Winston Churchill said during those pre-invasion days, 'It was the beginning of the end.'

Colonel Somerton, who had started our Home Guard, walked more slowly with his spaniel after the autumn partridges with his gun. He left us to live with relatives, his house was sold.

Alec Bradfield returned from brook clearing for the War Ag. to be the village roadman again. He and Skemer had seen so much happen over the last sixty years.

'Are we going to have council houses or be all our young chaps going to leave?' George Pitcher asked with anger at the annual parish meeting.

Howard Cambridge told us all that everything would work out in the end according to the Book of Ezekiel.

'It's now we want houses,' Harry White replied. 'Or else I'll have to move my family to Birmingham and live with my in-laws.'

'He can't do that, he's wanted on the railroad,' Laughing

Tom put in. 'What the Hanover are they doing at A'sum, not building houses for the parishioners?'

The evacuees were loth to return. The younger ones did, some who were older were courting and enjoying the green fields of Worcestershire. The older boys stayed and worked on the farms.

Men from Coventry took small holdings vacated by the natives.

Dad, who had been ailing for so long, slipped and broke his hip joint trying to build a garage. Who it was for I don't know, for he had given up driving some years before. He died and left a gap difficult to fill.

At No Gains Farm, Jim Hicks still pottered about with Sammy. Theirs were the most inquiring minds I knew; I won't say 'nosy', just concerned and afraid they wouldn't be first with the news. If a village girl became as they termed it in the family way, they said she had done the last job first or been to a whist drive.

Yes, there was mischief in Jim and Sammy but no real malice.

For didn't Sammy give Joyce and me a tablecloth for a wedding present, when linen was gold?

Having seen the land producing so little grain before Hitler forced the plough into our meadows with the submarine threat, and then the golden grain grow where before thistles pricked the sheep's noses on our hillside, I wondered how things would become normal again. What is normal anyway?

Sammy Bosworth sold his pigs and let his land to Mr. Bennet's successor, keeping just one orchard to graze about eight or ten ewes.

'Ho Ho Ho' his voice squeeched up over street as his ewes followed the bent little man with a little bag of sheep food.

'On the pension?' I said to Sammy.

'No, I've got a few too many coppers to draw that, but Jim Hicks, my man, has started to draw his now the war's over.'

Henry Fanshaw had gone now Mr. Bennet was dead.

'Yunt swift enough fur that Worcester chap?'

Jim grinned.

'How's that?' I said.

'Well, you knows what we allus said about Henry, he had got another gear to work in but it was a slower un. This bloke a bought a darn great diesel tractor on what they calls cater-pollars. He got a blade on the front known as a bulldozer.'

'What's Mr. Homes going to do then, Jim?' I asked.

Jim gave me a far away look and looked at the hawthorn hedges around the fields of No Gains Farm.

'See them hedges?' he said. 'He's a gwain to push un out with that yellow contraption and make one darn great field of the whole farm.'

I questioned the sense of it all.

Jim said, '1783 that was fenced off with hawthorn, what they called enclosures, to keep in the cattle and the like, and now its to hell with enclosures and steal every inch of ground where the cattle stood in the burra out of wind and sun and the little birds nested. He's only keeping Syd Freeman and Walt Gillet and a couple of young vacuees just leaving school.'

I looked at the hillside and saw Syd on the tractor with the bulldozer blade rip up the scene of centuries, push over the apple trees. Some land went to grow more wheat, some for grass to feed Walt Gillet's sheep and the cattle.

The hillside changed in a few months. Then Jim Hicks died one tea-time in March. In fact that winter had been severe, a winter that thinned the village of its old men and women.

'Didst ever know a man grow after he was dead?' Skemer asked me one day as I passed him sitting as usual on the slab over the tap at the roadside.

'No, why, Skemer,' I said. 'Who has then?'

'Oi, Jim Hicks was but five foot four, now his daughter a planted a long garden over him eight foot long. It grows bigger every time she tends the grave.'

I smiled at Skemer's whims.

Meat was still rationed and Laughing Tom was busy killing pigs in the winter time. I had a couple of sows, their litters of young were soon sold at eight weeks to the villagers to fatten for bacon.

The Government had promised that the War Ag. would go as soon as the war was over, but with subsidies for ditching and ploughing still operative the old order stayed.

Joe Smith gave up his farm. This was taken over by another Bulldozer Baron from Wolverhampton.

The whole village seemed different now the sense of urgency was gone.

We did have a return of whist drives and the man who bought Colonel Somerton's house started a Dramatic Society.

The new folk who came in wanted something more sophisticated than the recreation room to perform in. They didn't care for the stage being erected on a billiard table and the curtains never opening and closing at the right time. A fund was started to raise money for what was to be known as the Social Centre.

My friend Geoff returned after a spell in India following his escape at Dunkirk. He did not go back to the land but to a factory at Tewkesbury.

Geoff bought himself a new motor bike and didn't fancy working for low wages in the mud of winter and sun of summer on the fields he had ploughed and sown with horses in 1938.

So soon after the war the folk known as commuters flocked to our village to sleep in peace, drive a car and work in air-conditioned factories, making all the things we had been short of for so long.

My Massey Harris binder which Eric drew with his Fordson tractor was made too soon.

Tom Wheatcroft said, 'Same as I was, too soon,' he added, 'Get a new one, Fred bwoy, one with a power drive like that man up the road at Partridge Farm. I've seen him working. Makes a tidy shoove (sheaf) however thick the crop, the machine runs from the tractor engine.'

I had seen them, of course, but waited another harvest.

'They be cumbinning up Dumbleton road,' Skemer hissed at me through his teeth.

'Oi,' I said, 'how does that work?'

'Does all the blasted work at one go. They won't want no men on the land now, nor we shan't get any more decent bread.'

The machine, of course, cuts and threshes the grain and two men then tie the sacks as they fill. All the straw, chaff and rubbish falls in a swath at the back.

I watched the work, booked the contractor, and he came first into the nine-acre field called the Green Thurness.

The first combine to enter our village. My feelings were mixed as I stood on the deck of the machine with Dick and tied the two-hundredweight Midland Railways sacks, as they filled and let them down a slide of tin until they fell in rows on the long stubble.

Charles Stephenson, who did gentlemen's gardens, came to watch with Skemer.

They opened the sacks, took handfuls out, first sniffed at the grain, then bit the wheat between their teeth and spat it on the stubble.

''Tis soft,' Charles said. 'Not like it is from the thresher when it's mellowed and dried in the stook, then in the rick.'

I explained that the Government had a dryer to dry the grain at Stratford, then it would go to the Mill.

'Untidy job to me,' Skemer added. 'Just look at the length of the stubble. Tell that chap on the tractor to drop the cutting knife a feow inches and cut more straw.'

'The drum won't take it,' I said. 'Not at this pace, we've got another nine acres to do after tea.'

The Minneapolis Moline tractor and combine gorged the grain like a hungry monster and I had doubts about the stubble and the swath of straw and rubbish behind.

A new invention, another new invention, had arrived, the most important since fifty or sixty years ago, a knotter was fitted on the reaper which tied the sheaves instead of the women tying these by hand.

'It yunt perfect,' Skemer said. 'Thee wait and see how the stubble ploughs.'

It rained, we couldn't burn the straw or stubble and a green path of growing wheat grew from the grains which came over the back of the machine.

It looked bad but no longer were the stooks to stand like aisles in a church, or the threshing machine employ seven men to thresh the grain. The combine came to the fields where the bulldozer had cleared the hedges.

It seemed ironical that the men who once worked on the farms now made parts for the combine harvester, a machine which displaced labour.

Change had come to our village where once the broad-wheeled waggon rumbled in. Now this great contraption made of tin, but tomorrow was more important to me than to Skemer and Charles Stephenson. They had seen the end of the horse ploughing, the steam ploughing.

I had a young wife Joyce and a baby daughter Shelagh to work for. Tom Wheatcroft told me that every child a farmer's wife had, the farmer must plough one more furrow closer to the hedge to grow that bit of extra grain.

Saturday afternoon became more free and easy as Bennet's successor, Mr. Homes, used his bulldozer to level a field ready for the sound of the willow cricket bat to be heard as the ball whizzed for four at the Social Centre. Hard work it was to level the ridge and furrow land of the West Midlands, drain it and create a turf fit to play on.

Veteran Fred, who played in the old Eleven, as lissom behind the stumps as a county man, arranged Away games for us until the pitch was ready.

So Saturday afternoons in summer I drove my 1934 Austin twelve, and two more car owners took the rest of the team, and in a way things looked brighter with a wife and daughter at home.

It's true the village had changed; the old men who had bred and reared us were gone like old horses from a team.

As for me I often thought of the blind gypsy's words to George Borrow:

'Life is sweet, brother. There's night and day, brother, both sweet things; sun, moon and stars, brother, all sweet things; there's likewise a wind on the heath.'

FRED ARCHER

GOLDEN SHEAVES, BLACK HORSES

'Those who relish the human element in the countryside will thank Fred Archer for his latest book. I have enjoyed them all but this is probably the best – a simple narrative of village life in the countryside around Ashton Under Hill from 1880 to the turn of the century'

The Sunday Times

'A delight. For ripe rustic nostalgia Fred Archer leaves the field standing'

The Sunday Telegraph

'A wealth of period detail, well rounded characters and rich atmosphere – you can almost smell the plum blossom and the middens'

Manchester Evening News

CORONET BOOKS

ALSO BY FRED ARCHER

AND AVAILABLE IN CORONET

All these books are available at your local bookshop or newsagent, or can be ordered direct from the publisher. Just tick the titles you want and fill in the form below.

Prices and availability subject to change without notice.

....

CORONET BOOKS, P.O. Box 11, Falmouth, Cornwall.

Please send cheque or postal order, and allow the following for postage and packing:

U.K. — One book 19p plus 9p per copy for each additional book ordered, up to a maximum of 73p.

B.F.P.O. and EIRE — 19p for the first book plus 9p per copy for the next 6 books, thereafter 3p per book.

OTHER OVERSEAS CUSTOMERS — 20p for the first book and 10p per copy for each additional book.

Name..

Address..

....